Great Meals in Minutes was created by
Rebus, Inc.
and published by Time-Life Books.

Rebus, Inc.

Publisher: Rodney Friedman
Editorial Director: Shirley Tomkievicz

Editor: Marya Dalrymple
Art Director: Ronald Gross
Managing Editor: Brenda Goldberg
Senior Editor: Charles Blackwell
Food Editor and Food Stylist: Grace Young
Photographer: Steven Mays
Prop Stylist: Cathryn Schwing
Staff Writer: Alexandra Greeley
Associate Editor: Ann M. Harvey
Assistant Editor: Bonnie J. Slotnick
Assistant Food Stylist: Karen Hatt
Photography Assistant: Glenn Maffei
Recipe Tester: Gina Palombi Barclay
Production Assistant: Lorna Bieber

For information about any Time-Life book,
please write:
Reader Information
Time-Life Books
541 North Fairbanks Court
Chicago, Illinois 60611

Library of Congress Cataloging in Publication Data
Salad menus.
   (Great meals in minutes)
   Includes index.
   1. Salads. 2. Menus. 3. Cooks—United States—
Biography. I. Title: Time-Life Books. II. Series.
TX740.S267 1985   641.8′3   85-2733
ISBN 0-86706-261-4 (lib. bdg.)
ISBN 0-86706-260-6 (retail ed.)

Time-Life Books Inc.
is a wholly owned subsidiary of
Time Incorporated

Founder: Henry R. Luce 1898–1967
Editor-in-Chief: Henry Anatole Grunwald
President: J. Richard Munro
Chairman of the Board: Ralph P. Davidson
Corporate Editor: Jason McManus
Group Vice President, Books: Reginald K.
Brack Jr.
Vice President, Books: George Artandi

Time-Life Books Inc.

Editor: George Constable
Executive Editor: George Daniels
Editorial General Manager: Neal Goff
Director of Design: Louis Klein
Editorial Board: Dale M. Brown, Roberta
Conlan, Ellen Phillips, Gerry Schremp,
Gerald Simons, Rosalind Stubenberg,
Kit van Tulleken, Henry Woodhead
Director of Research: Phyllis K. Wise
Director of Photography: John Conrad Weiser

President: William J. Henry
Senior Vice President: Christopher T. Linen
Vice Presidents: Stephen L. Bair, Robert A.
Ellis, John M. Fahey Jr., Juanita T. James,
James L. Mercer, Joanne A. Pello, Paul R.
Stewart, Christian Strasser

Editorial Operations
Design: Ellen Robling (assistant director)
Copy Room: Diane Ullius
Editorial Operations: Caroline A. Boubin
(manager)
Production: Celia Beattie
Quality Control: James J. Cox (director),
Sally Collins
Library: Louise D. Forstall

SERIES CONSULTANT
Margaret E. Happel is the author of *Ladies
Home Journal Adventures in Cooking,
Ladies Home Journal Handbook of Holiday
Cuisine,* and other best-selling cookbooks, as
well as the translator and adapter of Rebecca
Hsu Hiu Min's *Delights of Chinese Cooking.*
A food consultant based in New York City,
she has been director of the food department
of *Good Housekeeping* and editor of
American Home magazine.

WINE CONSULTANT
Tom Maresca combines a full-time career
teaching English literature with writing
about and consuming fine wines. He is now
at work on *The Wine Case Book,* which
explains the techniques of wine tasting.

Cover: Jane Uetz's stuffed eggs tapénade,
tomato and melon salad with smoked ham,
and fried goat cheese with garlic bread. See
pages 33–35.

Great Meals
IN MINUTES
SALAD
MENUS

TIME
LIFE
BOOKS

TIME-LIFE BOOKS, ALEXANDRIA, VIRGINIA

Contents

Meet the Cooks

BRUCE AIDELLS

Early in his cooking career, Californian Bruce Aidells ran an on-campus restaurant at the University of California at Santa Cruz. Later, he was executive chef for the Poulet restaurant in Berkeley, where he prepared poultry in more than 500 different ways. He is now a restaurant consultant and teaches Louisiana-style cooking at the California Culinary Academy in San Francisco.

JANE UETZ

Jane Uetz began her cooking career in the test kitchens of a major food company in New York City. She later joined the staff of *American Home* magazine as associate food editor. Today, she is the director of the consumer and culinary center of a New York public relations agency. She also teaches cooking classes for business executives and appears on television and radio as a food and nutrition specialist.

MARY CARROLL DREMANN

A professional cook since 1971, Mary Carroll Dremann trained at schools and restaurants in the United States and in Europe. In 1983 she opened a retail cookware store, catering business, and cooking school, all under the name Cuisine Naturelle, in Mill Valley, California. She writes a monthly food column for the *Vegetarian Times* and the *Whole Life Times*.

VICTORIA WISE

Victoria Wise has been cooking professionally since 1971, when she left her graduate studies in philosophy to become the first chef at the Chez Panisse restaurant in Berkeley, California. She left Chez Panisse in 1973 to open a charcuterie, Pig by the Tail, in Berkeley, which she still operates.

CONNIE HANDA MOORE

Born in Seattle, Washington, to Japanese immigrants, Connie Handa Moore now lives in Princeton, New Jersey. She has worked as a caterer, food consultant, cooking teacher, and *sushi* chef. She is the owner of Handa Food Management, Inc., which operates the dining room at the Robert Wood Johnson Foundation in Princeton.

SUSAN HUBERMAN

Self-taught cook Susan Huberman catered executive lunches before becoming a freelance food stylist in 1974. Currently, she prepares and arranges food for television commercials and print advertising in New York City.

FRAN SHINAGEL AND DELORES CUSTER

As food stylists and home economists, Fran Shinagel and Delores Custer operate C/S Food Communications, a New York City consulting firm. Besides preparing food for print and film, they develop recipes for food companies and travel internationally as consultants to advertising firms. Together, they teach food styling at New York University and at the New School's Culinary Arts Restaurant School.

DEBORAH MADISON

Deborah Madison grew up in a farming community in central California. In 1979 she helped to found Greens, a vegetarian restaurant in San Francisco, where she also worked as head chef. She has taught cooking classes and catered in the Bay Area, and currently lives in Rome, where she cooks and studies Italian gardens.

ANNE LINDSAY GREER

A resident of Dallas, Texas, Anne Lindsay Greer is an authority on southwestern, or Tex-Mex, cooking. She is a frequent guest on television talk shows and radio broadcasts and is featured in the anthology *Cooking with the New American Chefs*. She writes for *Bon Appétit* and *The Pleasures of Cooking* and is the author of several cookbooks, including *Cuisine of the American Southwest*.

Salad Menus in Minutes
GREAT MEALS FOR FOUR IN AN HOUR OR LESS

Acclaimed for its versatility and ease of preparation, the salad has achieved new popularity in America now that a host of exciting ingredients have taken over the salad bowl. Arugula, radicchio, mâche, walnut and sesame oil, raspberry and balsamic vinegar, once considered exotic, are being used almost as widely as tomatoes and leaf lettuce. With salad bars springing up nationwide in restaurants, delicatessens, and supermarkets, Americans have accepted the fact that a salad can be a delicious main course and not simply the beginning or end of a meal. Today, salads combine vegetables, fruits, meats, poultry, cheese, tofu, pasta, and many other wholesome ingredients to provide a well-balanced alternative to a meat-and-potatoes meal.

The earliest salads consisted of greens dressed with little more than salt. In fact, the word "salad" derives from the Latin *sal*, meaning salt. Over the years, salads became increasingly more elaborate, reaching what might be considered a zenith at an Italian banquet in 1581 that featured "salads decked out with various fantasies such as animals made of citron, castles of turnips, high walls of lemons; and variegated with slices of ham, mullet roe, herrings, tunny, anchovies, capers, olives, caviar, together with candied flowers and other preserves." Salads are not nearly as formidable today, but salad making still offers cooks the opportunity to be creative with a wide range of ingredients.

On the following pages, nine of America's most talented cooks present 27 complete menus featuring all types of salads, from a simple BLT in a bowl to an unusual mixture of crabmeat and *shiitake* mushrooms served on a platter with jícama and red cabbage. There are also recipes for Italian, Chinese, Scandinavian, Japanese, Indian, Mexican, and French salads. Each menu, which serves four people, can be prepared in an hour or less. All call for fresh produce and top-quality fish, poultry, and meat, and many give directions for preparing homemade dressings. Additional ingredients (spices, herbs, and so on) are all of high quality and are available in supermarkets or specialty food stores.

The cooks and the kitchen staff have meticulously

Fresh vegetables, fruits, herbs, meat, and shellfish—the best from the market and garden—await the salad bowl. By mixing and matching tastes, colors, and textures, imaginative cooks can create an almost endless variety of quick and nourishing meals from these ingredients.

planned and tested the meals for appearance as well as for taste, as the accompanying photographs show: The vegetables and fruits are brilliant and fresh, the visual combinations appetizing. The table settings feature bright colors, simple flower arrangements, and attractive but not necessarily expensive serving dishes.

For each menu, the Editors, with advice from the cooks, suggest wines and other beverages. And there are suggestions for the use of leftovers and for complementary dishes and desserts. On each menu page, you will find a number of other tips, from an easy method for shelling and deveining shrimp to advice on choosing a ripe melon.

Because the salads in this volume contain so many different ingredients, specific vegetables, fruits, meats, fish, and poultry are discussed in the introductions to the various menus rather than on the following pages. Here you will find information on buying, preparing, and storing greens; on what to do with tofu; and on cooking several types of Oriental pasta. There are also sections on oils and vinegars, and some suggestions for the best ways to serve salads.

BEFORE YOU START
Great Meals in Minutes is designed for efficiency and ease. This book will work best for you if you follow these suggestions:

1. Read the guidelines on the following pages for selecting, storing, and preparing ingredients.

2. Refresh your memory with the few simple cooking techniques reviewed on pages 11–12. They will quickly become second nature and will help you to produce professional-quality meals in minutes.

3. Read the menus before you shop. Each lists the ingredients you will need, in the order that you would expect to shop for them. Many items will already be on your pantry shelf.

4. Check the equipment list on page 15. Good, sharp knives and pots and pans of the right shape and material are essential for making great meals in minutes. This may be the time to buy a few things. The right equipment can turn cooking from a necessity into a creative experience.

5. Set out everything you need before you start to cook: The lists at the beginning of each menu tell just what is required. To save effort, always keep your ingredients in the same place so you can reach for them instinctively.

6. Remove meat, fish, and eggs from the refrigerator early enough for them to reach room temperature.

7. Follow the start-to-finish steps for each menu. That

way, you can be sure of having the entire meal ready to serve in an hour.

GREENS

Various types of lettuce and other leafy green vegetables, such as spinach, arugula, and Belgian endive, are included in most salads. Ranging from sweet to bitter, greens can stand alone or in combination. Those listed alphabetically below are used in this volume; substitutes are noted in the individual recipes. For the best possible salad, choose greens carefully: Prime-quality greens should have full color, look fresh, and be free of insects, blemishes, or wilt. Avoid buying greens that look droopy; you will never be able to revive them at home.

Arugula: Also known as rocket, this fragile Italian green has small, flat leaves and a mustardy taste. Sold in bunches at specialty markets and Italian groceries, arugula should be used within three days of purchase.

Arugula

Belgian endive: Sold as compact heads that resemble plump cigars, this slightly bitter member of the chicory family originated in Belgium but today is being raised in this country as well. Belgian endive should be firm and very pale yellow to white. To keep it from discoloring, refrigerate it tightly wrapped in aluminum foil or waxed paper.

Belgian endive

Bibb lettuce: A premium lettuce usually grown in green-houses, Bibb has sweet, tender, dark green leaves that form a cup-shaped head. It is sold at quality greengrocers and some supermarkets.

Boston lettuce: Boston has tender leaves that form a furled crown. Both the pale green inner leaves and the darker outer leaves are sweet and delicate. It is available year round at supermarkets and greengrocers.

Boston lettuce

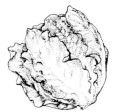

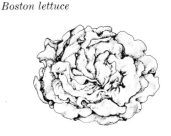

Bibb lettuce

Chicory: Sometimes called curly endive, chicory has narrow, serrated curly leaves that form a loosely bunched head. Because of its bitter taste and coarse texture, chicory is best combined with milder greens.

Chicory

Iceberg lettuce: One of the most widely available greens, versatile and sturdy iceberg has a very crisp leaf that adds a pleasant crunch to salads. The head should be round, light, and springy, and should give slightly when squeezed. Do not buy heads that feel hard or heavy or that have brown leaves—they are probably old and bitter. Iceberg keeps in the refrigerator for up to two weeks.

Mâche: Also called lamb's lettuce or corn salad, this green has fuzzy, elongated tongue-shaped leaves with a distinctive sweet taste. Available in fall and winter at specialty greengrocers, mâche is usually sold with its sandy roots attached and requires several washings. Highly perishable, it is best used within a day of purchase.

Radicchio: Native to Italy's Veneto province, this ruby red, purple-leaved chicory is highly prized for its beautiful color. It is available for only a few months during the winter season and, because it is imported, is costly. Look for *radicchio* at quality supermarkets and greengrocers or at Italian groceries.

Radicchio

Mâche

Red leaf lettuce: The mild-flavored, crisp-tender leaves of this popular lettuce are tipped with red and form a long loose-leafed bunch rather than a tight head. Its ruffled leaves highlight any salad.

Romaine lettuce: Also known as cos, this full-flavored sturdy lettuce has long, dark green outer leaves and pale inner leaves. Romaine is always used in Caesar salad (see page 82).

Romaine lettuce

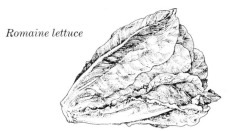

Spinach: This iron-rich vegetable is as popular raw as it is cooked. Sold loose and packaged at most supermarkets, quality spinach should have dark green leaves. Cut off the tough stems and midribs, and wash the leaves thoroughly before serving.

Sprouts: From tender alfalfa to crunchy mung bean, these protein-packed seedlings are sold loose from water-filled tubs or in plastic-wrapped containers and require only a light rinsing before use. They are available in many supermarkets, health food stores, and Oriental groceries and are easy to grow at home in special sprouters, a jar, or even on wet paper towels.

Watercress: Watercress is a peppery-tasting plant with long stems and small, round bright-green leaves. It makes an attractive garnish as well as a salad green. Avoid buying watercress that is even slightly yellow. Sold at most supermarkets and greengrocers, watercress should be used within several days of purchase.

Watercress

Washing and Storing Greens

To wash most varieties of lettuce, remove any wilted outer leaves, but keep the heads intact. If the variety is not too delicate, rinse the head under cold running water; otherwise, wash the head by swishing it in a sink or pan filled with cold water. Or, remove the leaves from the head altogether, then wash each leaf individually. Drain the heads, pull the leaves off if you haven't already, and dry them in a salad spinner, or dry each leaf gently and completely with paper towels.

Spinach is usually very gritty, even though the packaged type is often marked washed. Spinach leaves, whether loose or prepacked, should be rinsed in several changes of water. For arugula and watercress, cut off the stem ends, then untie the bunches before swishing in cold water. Dry spinach, arugula, and watercress as you would lettuce.

For convenience, some cooks favor washing greens immediately after purchase and storing them until needed. Many people, however, believe greens keep better unwashed. If you store greens unwashed, be sure to wash them at least an hour before serving, and then refrigerate until ready to use. No matter how you store greens, it is important that the leaves be dried well. Wrap the leaves in a kitchen towel or paper towel, then place them in a plastic bag in the vegetable crisper or on the bottom shelf of the refrigerator. If you store greens longer than a day, check them each day and replace the towel if it is damp.

Never store greens near apples, pears, cantaloupes, avocados, tomatoes, or plums; these fruits and vegetables emit ethylene gas as they ripen, which causes rusty-looking spots to appear on the leaves.

TOFU AND PASTA

Low in fat, tofu and pasta add texture to salads while acting as a foil for highly seasoned dressings and sauces. Tofu, or bean curd, is a protein-rich, ivory-colored soybean product. There are various types of tofu on the market, but for the recipes in this book, select the firm Chinese tofu sold in squares or pillow-shaped blocks in small plastic tubs. Firm Chinese tofu can be cut easily into cubes and retains its shape well when mixed with other ingredients. If you change the water in the tub daily, the tofu will last for a week in the refrigerator.

Pasta for salads should be cooked just until it is *al dente*, unless the recipe directions specify otherwise, or it will become gummy when combined with other ingredients. The less familiar pastas used in this volume are:

Chinese egg noodles: These dried or fresh noodles are made of eggs, wheat flour, and water, and are available in a number of thicknesses. The dried type are sold in cellophane packages in many supermarkets and last indefinitely. Fresh egg noodles will keep for up to a week in the

---

Making Chicken Stock

Although canned chicken broth or stock is all right for emergencies, homemade chicken stock has a rich flavor that is hard to match. Moreover, the commercial broths—particularly the canned ones—are likely to be oversalted.

To make your own stock, save chicken parts as they accumulate and put them in a bag in the freezer; then have a rainy-day stock-making session using one of the recipes below. The skin from a yellow onion will add color; the optional veal bone will add extra flavor and richness.

3 pounds bony chicken parts, such as wings, back, and neck
1 veal knuckle (optional)
3 quarts cold water
1 yellow unpeeled onion, stuck with 2 cloves
2 stalks celery with leaves, cut in 2
12 crushed peppercorns
2 carrots, scraped and cut into 2-inch lengths
4 sprigs parsley
1 bay leaf
1 tablespoon fresh thyme, or 1 teaspoon dried
Salt (optional)

1. Wash chicken parts and veal knuckle (if you are using it) and drain. Place in large soup kettle or stockpot (any big pot) with the remaining ingredients—except salt. Cover pot and bring to a boil over moderate heat.

2. Lower heat and simmer stock, partly covered, 2 to 3 hours. Skim foam and scum from top of stock several times. Add salt to taste after stock has cooked 1 hour.

3. Strain stock through fine sieve placed over large bowl. Discard chicken pieces, vegetables, and seasonings. Let stock cool uncovered (this will speed cooling process). When completely cool, refrigerate. Fat will rise and congeal conveniently at top. You may skim it off and discard it or leave it as protective covering for stock.

Yield: About 10 cups

refrigerator or for a month in the freezer. These noodles can be purchased at Oriental groceries.

Soba noodles: Made from buckwheat flour and gray-brown in color, these very thin dried Japanese noodles are round or flat. They are sold in health food stores and at Japanese groceries.

Udon noodles: Imported from Japan, *udon* noodles look like square spaghetti. Like *soba,* they are made from wheat, but they are white in color and are generally thicker than *soba* noodles. *Udon* noodles are available fresh or dried in some supermarkets and at Japanese groceries.

DRESSINGS

A good dressing is the soul of a salad: It binds the ingredients and enhances their flavors. Nothing can match the taste of a freshly made dressing prepared with good-quality ingredients, and homemade dressings cost less per serving than bottled varieties. Three types—the oil-vinegar mixture known as vinaigrette; mayonnaise, flavored and unflavored; and cream dressings—are the basis for dozens of improvisations. All of these dressings may be refrigerated but should not be frozen.

A basic vinaigrette usually combines three to four parts oil with one part vinegar or lemon juice and salt and pepper to taste. Garlic, shallots, mustard, and herbs can be added to the basic vinaigrette to give it more flavor. If you store vinaigrette in the refrigerator, the oil will thicken. Remove refrigerated vinaigrette at least an hour before you need it to bring it to room temperature, then whisk, taste, and re-season it if necessary.

Mayonnaise is a smooth emulsion of egg yolks (or whole eggs), oil, vinegar or lemon juice, and seasonings. Although many commercial varieties of mayonnaise are good—especially when mixed with lemon juice, sour cream, and olive oil—it is very easy to make your own mayonnaise by hand (see pages 90, 93) or in a blender or food processor (see page 12). You will find the difference appreciable.

Cream-based dressings generally consist of heavy cream or a tart cream such as sour cream, yogurt, or *crème fraîche,* mixed with lemon juice and herbs, if de-sired. Creamy dressings are particularly good on cabbage and potato salads.

You can make salad dressing several hours in advance of serving to amalgamate flavors, but be sure to shake or whisk it before adding it to the salad. For green salads, add the dressing just before serving or the vinegar and salt will make the greens limp. For salads made up of raw fruits and vegetables, blanched vegetables, tofu, grains, beans, or pasta, add the dressing well in advance of serving so it can be thoroughly absorbed. Never overdress any salad: Use just enough dressing to coat ingredients.

Oils

Olive oil, with its full flavor, is the oil of preference for making vinaigrettes and mayonnaise, but other, blander oils, such as the less expensive corn, peanut, safflower, and blended vegetable oils, are also suitable. Unopened, oils keep indefinitely; once opened, they should be stored in a cool, dark place or in the refrigerator. Although refrigerated oil keeps longer, it may become thick and slightly cloudy, so allow time for it to come to room temperature before using. Taste an oil before putting it into a dressing to make sure it has not become rancid. The following oils are included in this book:

Olive oil: The highest-quality olive oil, extra-virgin, is fine-flavored, aromatic—and expensive. It is worth the extra cost, however, because its bouquet and flavor will enhance many types of salads. If you use one of the other grades (superfine virgin and fine virgin are also good), be sure to choose a clear, fragrant product.

Oriental sesame oil: This amber to dark brown oil, redolent of toasted sesame seeds, is a key ingredient in Oriental dressings. Look for sesame oil in the Oriental food section of your supermarket or in a Chinese or Japanese grocery. Light-colored Middle Eastern-style sesame oil is mild flavored and not a good substitute.

Safflower oil: This light polyunsaturated golden oil is made from the seeds of a thistle-like herb whose leaves are often used in Indian dishes. Safflower oil is fine for dressing complex and highly seasoned salads.

Peanut oil: Domestic peanut oils, preferred in this book, are highly refined and do not have a pronounced peanut flavor. French and Chinese peanut oils are stronger and not particularly good on salads.

Vinegars

The word "vinegar" derives from the French words *vin aigre*, meaning sour wine—appropriate since the earliest vinegars were made only from wine. Today, vinegars are produced from fermented apple cider, distilled cereal grains, rice wine, and many other sources. They may be plain or flavored with herbs, spices, flower petals, or fruit. Flavored vinegars may not appeal to all tastes, but they add an extra dimension to dressings.

Vinegars vary in strength, or bite, depending on their acid content. The color of vinegars also varies from clear to dark brown, but regardless of the hue, the product should not be cloudy and should have a pleasant (though sometimes pungent) aroma. The recipes in this volume use the following vinegars:

Red and white wine vinegar: These versatile, unflavored vinegars are the traditional ingredient in most vinegar-based dressings. A French or Italian import or a domestic vinegar produced by traditional methods is markedly more flavorful than a mass-produced brand.

Tarragon vinegar: This white wine vinegar is flavored with fresh tarragon leaves. To make your own, add 2 cups fresh tarragon to 1 quart white wine vinegar, bring to a boil, then cool and let stand in covered bottles at room temperature for two weeks. Strain, rebottle, and seal.

Raspberry vinegar: Another white wine vinegar, this newly popular product is flavored with raspberries. Look for it wherever gourmet foods are sold, or, if you prefer, make your own raspberry vinegar by simmering 2 cups of fresh raspberries in 1 quart of white wine vinegar for 10 minutes. Pour this mixture into a jar, cover, and let stand in a cool place for two weeks. Strain it into bottles and seal.

Apple cider vinegar: This delightful vinegar has mild apple overtones and, when properly aged, an amber color. The combination of many apple varieties gives it an intriguing taste. Look for top-quality cider vinegar in health food stores, specialty food shops, and apple orchard outlet stores; it is far superior to the brands usually found in supermarkets.

Balsamic vinegar: A dark, sweet-and-sour, rather expensive wine vinegar produced only in Modena, Italy, balsamic vinegar is aged for at least three, and up to fifty, years. Intensely aromatic, it is so mellow you can use it as a dressing without the addition of oil, or it can be combined with other vinegars. Purchase it at well-stocked supermarkets and gourmet shops.

Chinese black vinegar: Dark brown, with a sweet flavor, this product is made from fermented rice and is similar in taste to balsamic vinegar. It complements very sweet or rich ingredients. Black vinegar is inexpensive and can be found in Oriental markets.

SERVING A SALAD

Deep bowls are good for leafy salads; shallow platters show off mixed and composed salads to best advantage. In some instances, particularly when you want a formal look, you may want to serve a salad or salads already arranged on individual plates.

Salad bowls come in many different sizes and materials—wood, china, porcelain, pottery, plastic, and glass, to name a few. Of these, wood is the most traditional, but if you use it, some precautions should be taken, particularly if you are using an unvarnished bowl. Because unvarnished wood is porous, it absorbs oil that can turn rancid if the bowl is wiped out rather than washed. A quick rinsing with soap and water is all that is needed; do not soak wood or put the bowl into a dishwasher. Clear plastic or glass bowls are easy to clean and show off the salad from all sides. Avoid metal bowls because the acid in the dressing discolors them and they may give a metallic taste to the salad. The proper size bowl for a green salad for four should have about a two-gallon capacity. If you are serving a cold salad, chill the bowl or plates prior to mealtime.

As salad servers, blunt wooden tools are recommended because, unlike metal or plastic implements, they do not have sharp edges that can bruise greens.

GENERAL COOKING TECHNIQUES

A number of the salads and side dishes in this volume include meats and vegetables cooked by the following methods:

Sautéing

Sautéing is a form of quick frying with no cover on the pan. In French, *sauter* means "to jump," which is what vegetables or small pieces of food do when you shake the sauté pan. The purpose is to brown the food lightly and seal in the juices, sometimes before further cooking. This technique has three critical elements: the right pan, the proper temperature, and dry food.

The sauté pan: A proper sauté pan is 10 to 12 inches in diameter and has 2- to 3-inch straight sides that allow you to turn the food and still keep the fat from spattering. It has a heavy bottom that can be moved back and forth easily across a burner.

The best material (and the most expensive) for a sauté pan is tin-lined copper because it is a superior heat conductor. Heavy-gauge aluminum works well but will discolor acidic food like tomatoes. Therefore, you should not use aluminum if acidic food is to be cooked for more than 20 minutes after the initial browning. Another option is to select a heavy-duty sauté pan made of strong, heat-conducting aluminum alloys. This type of professional cookware is smooth and stick resistant.

Use a sauté pan large enough to hold the food without crowding, or sauté in two batches. The heat of the fat and the air spaces around and between the pieces facilitate browning.

Many recipes call for sautéing first, then lowering the heat and cooking the food, covered, for an additional 10 to 20 minutes. Be sure you buy a sauté pan with a tight-fitting cover. Make certain the handle is long and is comfortable to hold. Use a wooden spatula or tongs to keep

Blender or Food Processor Mayonnaise

Making mayonnaise is an easy technique to master and one that good cooks should learn. Before the advent of the blender and food processor, mayonnaise was made by hand, and many people still prefer this method (see Deborah Madison's recipes for handmade mayonnaise on pages 90, 93). However, with these appliances, you can produce mayonnaise in seconds. Remember, any machine-made mayonnaise requires a whole egg, not just the yolk; otherwise, the dressing will be too stiff. Homemade mayonnaise will keep for a week in the refrigerator.

2 whole eggs, at room temperature
½ teaspoon salt
½ teaspoon dry mustard
1 to 1¼ cups olive oil or vegetable oil, according
   to preference
2 tablespoons freshly squeezed lemon juice

1. Combine eggs, salt, and mustard in blender or food processor and blend at low speed until combined.
2. With machine running, slowly drizzle in ½ cup oil. Gradually add lemon juice.
3. With machine still running, slowly add remaining oil until mayonnaise has reached desired consistency.

Yield: 1¾ cups

food moving in the pan as you shake it over the burner. If the food sticks, as it occasionally will, a metal spatula will loosen it best. Turn the food so that all surfaces come into contact with the hot fat.

Never immerse the hot pan in cold water because this will warp the metal. Allow the pan to cool slightly, then add water and let it sit until you are ready to wash it.

The fat: Half butter and half vegetable or peanut oil is perfect for most sautéing: It heats to high temperatures without burning, yet gives a rich butter flavor. For cooking, unsalted butter tastes best and adds no extra salt.

Some sautéing recipes in this book call for olive oil, which imparts a delicious and distinctive flavor of its own and is less sensitive than butter to high heat. Nevertheless, even the finest olive oil has some residue of fruit pulp, which will occasionally scorch. Watch carefully when you sauté in olive oil; discard any scorched oil and start with fresh, if necessary.

To sauté properly, heat the fat until it is hot but not smoking. When you see small bubbles on top of the fat, lower the heat because it is on the verge of smoking. When using butter and oil together, add butter to the hot oil. After the foam from the melting butter subsides, you are ready to sauté. If the temperature of the fat is just right, the food will sizzle when you put it in the pan. Bruce Aidells sautés *andouille* sausage for his Creole-style Potato Salad, page 25.

Stir Frying

The basic cooking method for Chinese cuisine, this fast-cook technique requires very little oil, and the foods—which you stir continuously—fry quickly over very high heat. Stir frying is ideal for cooking bite-size, shredded, or thinly sliced portions of vegetables, fish, meat, or poultry, alone or in combination. Connie Handa Moore stir fries strips of beef, page 62.

Deep Frying

This technique is known in almost every nation and in some ways is similar to stir frying. You immerse small batches of food cut into small pieces in very hot oil until crisp on the outside and cooked through within.

Because the temperature of the oil for deep frying is critical, a deep-fat thermometer is a must. As you gain experience in deep frying, however, you will be able to gauge the temperature by the appearance of the oil or by testing a bit of food. At 275 degrees, the oil has small swirls and subsurface eddies but is not bubbling, and a small piece of food dropped into the pan will sink to the bottom and begin cooking at once. At 375 degrees, the oil gives off a slight haze, and food added at this time will rise to the top, surrounded by bubbles. At 400 degrees—the temperature for a very quick fry—the oil is just below the smoking point and gives off a thicker haze. A piece of food will rise quickly to the surface, covered by white foam, and will brown immediately. Do not linger or the oil may burn. Begin cooking at once. Anne Lindsay Greer deep fries strips of corn tortillas, page 100.

Blanching

Also called parboiling, blanching is an invaluable technique. Immerse whole or cut vegetables or other foods for a few minutes in boiling water, then refresh them, that is, plunge them into cold water to stop their cooking and set their colors. Blanching softens or tenderizes dense or crisp vegetables, often as a preliminary to further cooking by another method, such as stir frying. Bruce Aidells blanches strips of squid, page 19.

Steaming

Steaming is a fast and nutritious way to cook vegetables and other food. Bring water to a boil in a saucepan. Place the food in a steamer or on a rack over the liquid and cover the pan, periodically checking the water level. Keeping the food above the liquid preserves vitamins and minerals often lost in other methods of cooking. Susan Huberman steams carrots and zucchini, pages 69–70.

Glazing

Glazing foods in their cooking liquid, butter or oil, and a little sugar gives them a slight sheen as the ingredients reduce to a syrupy consistency. Glazing enhances the foods' flavor and appearance, and they need no additional sauce. Connie Handa Moore glazes beef and mushrooms in her Menu 3, page 61.

Broiling and Grilling

In broiling, the food cooks directly under the heat source. In grilling, the food cooks either directly over an open fire or on a well-seasoned cast-iron or stoneware griddle placed directly over a burner. Susan Huberman broils bell peppers to aid in removing their skins, page 69.

Pantry (for this volume)

A well-stocked, properly organized pantry is essential for preparing great meals in the shortest time possible. Whether your pantry consists of a small refrigerator and two or three shelves over the sink, or a large freezer, refrigerator, and entire room just off the kitchen, you must protect staples from heat and light.

In maintaining your pantry, follow these rules:

1. Store staples by kind and date. Canned goods, canisters, and spices need a separate shelf, or a separate spot on a shelf. Date all staples—shelved, refrigerated, or frozen—by writing the date directly on the package or on a bit of masking tape. Then put the oldest ones in front to be sure you use them first.

2. Store flour, sugar, and other dry ingredients in canisters or jars with tight lids. Glass and clear plastic allow you to see at a glance how much remains.

3. Keep a running grocery list so that you can note when a staple is half gone, and be sure to stock up.

ON THE SHELF:

Anchovies
Anchovy fillets, both flat and rolled, come oil-packed, in tins. If you buy whole, salt-packed anchovies, they must be cleaned under running water, skinned, and boned. To bone, separate the fish with your fingers and slip out the backbone.

Baking powder

Capers
Capers are usually packed in vinegar and less frequently in salt. If you use the latter, you should rinse them under cold water before using them.

Flour
all-purpose, bleached or unbleached

Garlic
Store in a cool, dry, well-ventilated place. Garlic powder and garlic salt are not adequate substitutes for fresh garlic.

Herbs and spices
The flavor of fresh herbs is much better than that of dried. Fresh herbs should be refrigerated and used as soon as possible. The following herbs are perfectly acceptable dried, but buy in small amounts, store airtight in dry area away from heat and light, and use as quickly as possible. In measuring herbs, remember that one part dried will equal three parts fresh. *Note:* Dried chives and parsley should not be on your shelf, since they have little or no flavor; frozen chives are acceptable. Buy whole spices rather than ground, as they keep their flavor much longer. Grind spices at home and store as directed for herbs.

basil
bay leaves
Cayenne pepper
cinnamon
coriander, whole and
    ground
cumin seeds, whole and
    ground
curry powder
dill
marjoram
mustard
oregano
paprika
pepper
> *black peppercorns*
> These are unripe peppercorns dried in their husks. Grind with a pepper mill for each use.
> *white peppercorns*
> These are the same as the black variety, but are picked ripe and husked. Use them in pale sauces when black pepper specks would spoil the appearance.
rosemary
salt
> Use coarse salt—commonly available as kosher or sea—for its superior flavor, texture, and purity. Kosher salt and sea salt are less salty than table salt. Substitute in the following proportions: three-quarters teaspoon table salt equals just under one teaspoon kosher or sea salt.
tarragon
thyme
turmeric

Honey

Hot pepper sauce

Nuts, whole, chopped, or
    slivered
almonds
pecans
pine nuts (pignoli)
walnuts

Oils
corn, safflower, peanut,
    or vegetable
> Because these neutral-tasting oils have high smoking points, they are good for high-heat sautéing.
olive oil
> Sample French, Greek, Spanish, and Italian oils. Olive oil ranges in color from pale yellow to dark green and in taste from mild and delicate to rich and fruity. Different olive oils can be used for different purposes: for example, stronger ones for cooking, lighter ones for salads. The finest quality olive oil is labeled extra-virgin or virgin.
sesame oil
> Dark amber-colored Oriental-style oil, used for seasoning; do not substitute light cold-pressed sesame oil.

Olives
California pitted black olives

Niçoise, Gaeta, or Kalamata olives

Onions
Store all dry-skinned onions in a cool, dry, well-ventilated place.
red or Italian onions
> Zesty tasting and generally eaten raw. The perfect salad onion.
shallots
> The most subtle member of the onion family, the shallot has a delicate garlic flavor.
yellow onions
> All-purpose cooking onions, strong in taste.

Pasta and noodles, dried
    or fresh
Chinese egg noodles
Fusilli, green and white

Potatoes, boiling and
    baking
> "New" potatoes are not a particular kind of potato, but any potato that has not been stored.

Rice
long-grain white rice
> Slender grains, much longer than they are wide, that become light and fluffy when cooked and are best for general use.

Sesame seeds

Soy Sauce
Japanese
> Lighter and less salty than Chinese and American brands.

Stock, chicken
> For maximum flavor and quality, your own stock is best (see recipe page 9),

but canned stock, or broth, is adequate for most recipes and convenient to have on hand.

Sugar

granulated sugar

Tomatoes

Italian plum tomatoes
Canned plum tomatoes (preferably imported) are an acceptable substitute for fresh.

Vinegars

apple cider vinegar
balsamic vinegar
distilled white vinegar
raspberry vinegar
rice vinegar
red and white wine
vinegars
sherry vinegar
tarragon vinegar

Wines and spirits

sherry, dry
white wine, dry

Water chestnuts

Worcestershire sauce

IN THE REFRIGERATOR:

Basil

Though fresh basil is widely available only in summer, try to use it whenever possible to replace dried; the flavor is markedly superior. Stand the stems, preferably with roots intact, in a jar of water, and loosely cover leaves with a plastic bag.

Bread crumbs

You need never buy bread crumbs. To make fresh crumbs, use fresh or day-old bread and process in food processor or blender. For dried, toast bread 30 minutes in preheated 250-degree oven, turning occasionally to prevent slices from browning. Proceed as for fresh. Store bread crumbs in an airtight container: fresh crumbs in the refrigerator and dried crumbs in a cool, dry place. Either type may also be frozen for several weeks if tightly wrapped in a plastic bag.

Butter

Many cooks prefer unsalted butter because of its finer flavor and because it does not burn as easily as salted.

Buttermilk

Cheese

Goat cheese
Goat cheese, or *chèvre*, has a distinct tanginess, though it is quite mild when young. Domestic goat cheeses are less salty than the imported types.

Jarlsberg
This firm Norwegian cheese resembles Swiss but is slightly sweeter. A slight gleam should be visible in the eyes, or holes.

Monterey Jack cheese
From California—a mild cheese made from skim, partly skim, or whole milk. Ideal for cooking, eating, and grating.

Parmesan cheese
Avoid the pre-grated packaged variety; it is very expensive and almost flavorless. Buy Parmesan by the quarter- or half-pound wedge and grate as needed: 4 ounces produces about one cup of grated cheese.

Chives

Refrigerate fresh chives wrapped in plastic. You may also buy small pots of growing chives—keep them on a windowsill and snip as needed.

Coriander

Also called *cilantro* or Chinese parsley, its pungent leaves resemble flat-leaf parsley. Keep in a glass of water covered with a plastic bag.

Cream

heavy cream
sour cream

Eggs

Will keep 4 to 5 weeks in refrigerator. For best results, bring to room temperature before using, except when separating.

Ginger, fresh

Found in the produce section. Wrap in a paper towel, then in plastic, and refrigerate; it will keep for about 1 month, but should be checked weekly for mold. Or, if you prefer, store it in the freezer, where it will last about 3 months. Firm, smooth-skinned ginger need not be peeled.

Lemons

In addition to its many uses in cooking, a slice of lemon rubbed over cut apples and pears will keep them from discoloring. Do not substitute bottled juice or lemon extract.

Limes

Mayonnaise

Although commercially prepared mayonnaise is adequate for most recipes, homemade has a better flavor, and you can make it quickly and easily (see recipe page 12).

Milk

Mint

Fresh mint will keep for a week if wrapped in a damp paper towel and enclosed in a plastic bag.

Miso, white

This flavorful paste of fermented soy and rice (called *shiromiso* in Japanese) will keep for three months in the refrigerator.

Mustards

The recipes in this book usually call for Dijon or coarse-grained mustard.

Parsley

The two most commonly available kinds of parsley are flat-leaf and curly; they can be used interchangeably when necessary. Flat-leaf parsley has a more distinctive flavor and is generally preferred in cooking. Curly parsley wilts less easily and is excellent for garnishing. Store parsley in a glass of water and cover loosely with a plastic bag. It will keep for a week in the refrigerator. Or wash and dry it, and refrigerate in a small plastic bag with a dry paper towel inside to absorb any moisture.

Scallions

Scallions have a mild onion flavor. Store wrapped in plastic.

Tofu

Recipes in this volume call for firm Chinese-style tofu.

Yogurt

Equipment

Proper cooking equipment makes the work light and is a good cook's most prized possession. You can cook expertly without a store-bought steamer or even a food processor, but basic pans, knives, and a few other items are indispensable. Below are the things you need—and some attractive options—for preparing the menus in this volume.

Pots and pans
Large kettle or stockpot
3 skillets (large, medium, small) with covers; one with oven-proof handle
2 heavy-gauge sauté pans, 10 to 12 inches in diameter, with covers
3 saucepans with covers (1-, 2-, and 4-quart capacities)
  Choose heavy-gauge enameled cast-iron, plain cast-iron, aluminum-clad stainless steel, or aluminum (but you need at least one saucepan that is not aluminum). Best—but very expensive—is tin-lined copper.
Nonaluminum double boiler
Roasting pan with rack
Shallow baking pan (13 x 9 x 2-inch)
Cookie sheet
12-cup muffin pan
9-inch pie pan
Large ovenproof baking dish
Ovenproof serving platters
Salad bowl

Knives
  A carbon-steel knife takes a sharp edge but tends to rust. You must wash and dry it after each use; otherwise it can blacken foods and counter tops. Good-quality stainless-steel knives, frequently honed, are less trouble and will serve just as well in the home kitchen. Never put a fine knife in the dishwasher. Rinse it, dry it, and put it away—but not loose in a drawer. Knives will stay sharp if they have their own storage rack.
10-inch chef's knife
Bread knife (serrated edge)
Small paring knife
Sharpening steel

Other cooking tools
2 sets of mixing bowls in graduated sizes, one set preferably glass or stainless steel
Colander with a round base (stainless steel, aluminum, or enamel)
2 sieves in fine and coarse mesh
2 strainers in fine and coarse mesh
2 sets of measuring cups and spoons in graduated sizes
  One for dry ingredients, another for shortenings and liquids.
Mesh strainer
Cooking spoon
Slotted spoon
Long-handled wooden spoons
Ladle
2 metal spatulas or turners (for lifting hot foods from pans)
Slotted spatula
Fork (for combining ingredients)
Rubber or vinyl spatula (for folding in ingredients)
Grater (metal, with several sizes of holes)
  A rotary grater is handy for hard cheese.
Small wire whisk
Pair of metal tongs
Wooden board
Garlic press
Vegetable peeler
Vegetable brush
Pastry brush for basting (a small, new paintbrush that is not nylon serves well)
Cooling rack
Deep-fat thermometer
Kitchen shears
Kitchen timer
Cheesecloth
Aluminum foil
Paper towels
Plastic wrap
Waxed paper
Brown paper bag
Kitchen string
Oven mitts or potholders

Electric appliances
Food processor or blender
  A blender will do most of the work required in this volume, but a food processor will do it more quickly and in larger volume. A food processor should be considered a necessity, not a luxury, for anyone who enjoys cooking.
Electric mixer

Optional cooking tools
Salad spinner
Melon baller
Spice grinder
Salad servers
Citrus juicer
  Inexpensive glass kind from the dime store will do.
Zester
Roll of masking tape or white paper tape for labeling and dating

Bruce Aidells

MENU 1 (Right)
Calamari Vinaigrette
Asparagus Wrapped in Prosciutto
Mushroom, Provolone, and Radish Salad

MENU 2
Chinese Egg Vermicelli with
Vegetables and Ham
Cold Beef Salad with Ginger Dressing

MENU 3
Meat and Vegetable Salad
Creole-style Potato Salad with Sausage
Romaine Lettuce and Tomatoes with
Blue Cheese and Anchovy Dressing

Bruce Aidells is an enthusiastic cook who describes his food as substantial and lavishly seasoned, often with a generous amount of garlic. He likes to experiment with Italian, Chinese, and Louisiana Creole recipes, creating menus that are colorful as well as flavorful. He finds that serving two or three salads in one meal is a good way to mix and match tastes and textures, while providing nutritional balance.

The three cold salads of Menu 1 were inspired by his memories of meals he ate from the *antipasti* carts in Italy. Like most Italian dishes, these salads do not require elaborate garnishing to be appealing. A crusty loaf of Italian or French bread is all that is needed to complete this springtime lunch or dinner.

For the Chinese-style salads of Menu 2, Bruce Aidells combines vegetables and flavorings common to Chinese cooking with meats popular in this country. Both salads are adaptable. For example, the cook suggests substituting Chinese barbecued pork *(char su),* if you can find it, for the smoky Westphalian ham in the vermicelli salad. And lean pork or dark-meat chicken or turkey can be used in the beef salad.

Inspired by French, English, Spanish, African, and native American cuisines, Menu 3 features a hot potato salad spiced with Creole mustard and Louisiana *andouille* sausage. With it, the cook serves a salad of cold meat and vegetables, and another consisting of romaine lettuce and tomato wedges tossed with a blue cheese and anchovy dressing.

Elegant prosciutto-wrapped asparagus spears, topped with a shallot and mustard dressing, accompany chilled calamari *vinaigrette. For this informal meal, serve the sliced mushrooms, radishes, and provolone cheese on individual salad plates.*

16

Calamari Vinaigrette
Asparagus Wrapped in Prosciutto
Mushroom, Provolone, and Radish Salad

Squid (*calamari* in Italian) is available in many parts of the country, especially at Italian or Oriental fish markets. Although fresh squid is not sold live, it should look moist, have creamy white flesh partially covered with a patchy mauve membrane, and no sour or fishy odor. Most often squid is sold frozen in blocks. To thaw it, place the frozen squid in its original wrapping in a deep pan in the refrigerator. It should be ready to cook in about 24 hours. For the *calamari* vinaigrette, the squid is blanched quickly and then marinated in a mildly seasoned dressing.

Prosciutto is an Italian-style dry-cured unsmoked ham, usually eaten raw. Top-quality prosciutto is deep pink, moist, and not overly salty. If it is not available, substitute Westphalian ham. Select smooth-skinned asparagus that are plump and bright green, with compact tips; open, leafy tips are a sure sign of age. Round, thick spears are usually more tender than thin or flat ones. Before storing the asparagus, cut a small piece from the bottom of each spear, then stand the spears upright in a container of cold water in the refrigerator. They should stay fresh for several days.

WHAT TO DRINK

In Italy, bright acidic dishes like these would be well matched with an equally bright acidic white wine like Pinot Grigio, or with a more supple, accommodating one like Soave.

SHOPPING LIST AND STAPLES

2 pounds small squid
12 thin slices prosciutto (about ½ pound total weight)
12 large asparagus spears (about 1 pound total weight)·
½ pound mushrooms
2 small red bell peppers
Small green bell pepper
1 bunch red radishes
Small red onion
Small bunch scallions
2 shallots
3 cloves garlic
2 bunches parsley
Small bunch fresh oregano, or 1 tablespoon dried

Small bunch fresh basil, marjoram, or chervil, or 2 teaspoons dried herbs if not using fresh oregano
2 lemons
½ pint sour cream or crème fraîche
¼ pound provolone cheese, preferably imported
1¾ cups olive oil
2 tablespoons raspberry vinegar, preferably, or red wine vinegar
2 tablespoons red wine vinegar, plus 2 tablespoons if not using raspberry vinegar
2 tablespoons Dijon mustard
Pinch of sugar
Salt and freshly ground black pepper

UTENSILS

Food processor or blender
Large skillet with tight-fitting cover
Large saucepan
2 large bowls
Medium-size bowl
Small bowl
Colander
Measuring cups and spoons
Chef's knife
Paring knife
2 wooden spoons
Rubber spatula
Whisk
Juicer

START-TO-FINISH STEPS

1. Peel and mince garlic for calamari, asparagus, and mushroom salad recipes. Peel and finely chop shallots for asparagus recipe. Wash and dry parsley, and fresh herbs if using. Finely chop enough parsley to measure ¾ cup for calamari, asparagus, and mushroom salad recipes. Finely chop enough oregano to measure ¼ cup for calamari recipe and enough oregano or other herb to measure 2 tablespoons for mushroom salad recipe.
2. Follow calamari recipe steps 1 through 11.
3. Follow mushroom salad recipe steps 1 through 4.
4. Follow asparagus recipe steps 1 through 4 and mushroom salad recipe steps 5 through 7.
5. Follow asparagus recipe steps 5 through 7, mushroom salad recipe step 8, and serve with calamari.

RECIPES

Calamari Vinaigrette

1 tablespoon salt
2 pounds small squid
2 small red bell peppers
Small green bell pepper
2 scallions
Small red onion
½ cup finely chopped parsley

Vinaigrette:
2 lemons
1 tablespoon minced garlic
2 teaspoons salt
1 teaspoon freshly ground black pepper
¼ cup finely chopped fresh oregano, or 1 tablespoon dried
1 cup olive oil

1. In large saucepan, combine 3 quarts water and 1 tablespoon salt and bring to a boil over high heat.
2. Meanwhile, fill large bowl half full with ice water.
3. Halve squid lengthwise and remove quill-like piece located at top of body sac. Rinse squid thoroughly under cold running water and cut each half lengthwise into 2 strips.
4. Plunge squid into boiling water for 20 seconds, or just until opaque. Immediately turn into colander and transfer to bowl of ice water; set aside.
5. Wash and dry red and green bell peppers. Core, halve, seed, and quarter peppers. Cut each quarter crosswise into ⅛-inch-wide strips; set aside in medium-size bowl.
6. Wash scallions and dry with paper towels. Trim off ends and discard. Chop scallions finely and place in bowl with peppers.
7. Halve onion, reserving one half for another use. Peel and finely dice remaining half; add to bowl. Add chopped parsley and set aside.
8. Squeeze enough lemon juice to measure ¼ cup.
9. Turn chilled squid into colander to drain; dry with paper towels. Rinse and dry large bowl.
10. For vinaigrette, combine lemon juice, garlic, salt, pepper, oregano, and oil in large bowl and beat with fork until blended.
11. Add squid and chopped ingredients to vinaigrette and toss until evenly coated. Cover bowl with plastic wrap and refrigerate until ready to serve.

Asparagus Wrapped in Prosciutto

2 teaspoons salt
12 large asparagus spears (about 1 pound total weight)
12 thin slices prosciutto (about ½ pound total weight)
½ teaspoon minced garlic
2 tablespoons finely chopped shallots
2 tablespoons raspberry vinegar, preferably, or red wine vinegar
1 tablespoon Dijon mustard
2 tablespoons finely chopped parsley
6 tablespoons olive oil

1. Combine 1 quart water and salt in large skillet and bring to a boil over high heat.
2. Meanwhile, snap off tough woody bottoms of asparagus. Peel stalks, if desired, and rinse under cold running water.
3. Add asparagus to boiling water in a single layer. Cover skillet and cook about 6 minutes, or just until asparagus are tender when pricked with point of a knife.
4. Turn cooked asparagus into colander and immediately refresh under cold running water; set aside to drain.
5. Pat asparagus dry with paper towels. Wrap each spear from stem to just below tip with a slice of prosciutto. Divide asparagus among 4 dinner plates; set aside.
6. For dressing, combine garlic, shallots, vinegar, mustard, and parsley in small bowl. Whisking continuously, add olive oil in a slow, steady stream and stir until dressing is well blended and creamy.
7. Spoon dressing over asparagus and serve.

Mushroom, Provolone, and Radish Salad

½ pound mushrooms
1 bunch red radishes
¼ pound provolone cheese, preferably imported
2 tablespoons finely chopped parsley
1 tablespoon Dijon mustard
2 tablespoons red wine vinegar
Pinch of sugar
1 teaspoon minced garlic
2 tablespoons finely chopped fresh oregano, basil, marjoram or chervil, or 2 teaspoons dried
6 tablespoons olive oil
¼ cup sour cream or crème fraîche

1. Wipe mushrooms clean with damp paper towels. Slice thinly and place in large bowl.
2. Wash radishes under cold running water and dry with paper towels. Slice thinly to measure about 1¼ cups and add to bowl with mushrooms.
3. Cut cheese into 2-inch-long by ⅛-inch-wide strips and add to sliced vegetables.
4. Add parsley to bowl with vegetables and cheese and toss to combine. Cover with plastic wrap and refrigerate until ready to serve.
5. For dressing, combine mustard, vinegar, sugar, garlic, and herbs in food processor or blender, and process briefly to combine.
6. With machine running, add oil in a slow, steady stream, and process until thick and creamy, scraping down sides of container as necessary.
7. With machine off, add sour cream or crème fraîche. Turn machine on and off until ingredients are blended; set aside.
8. Pour dressing over vegetables and cheese and toss until evenly coated. Divide among 4 salad plates and serve.

Chinese Egg Vermicelli with Vegetables and Ham
Cold Beef Salad with Ginger Dressing

The vermicelli salad includes three ingredients often used in Chinese cooking—Chinese egg noodles (for more information, see page 9), snow peas, and dried black mushrooms. The snow peas should be crisp and bright green, with the tiny peas just visible inside. To store the pods, refrigerate them unwashed in a perforated plastic bag; they will last four to five days. If you must use frozen snow peas, blanch them just until they are heated through; otherwise, they become soggy.

Dried Chinese black mushrooms have a characteristic

Two chilled salads—vermicelli with vegetables and ham, and beef with ginger dressing—make an impressive buffet lunch or supper. For an authentic touch, offer your guests the option of using chopsticks.

meaty flavor. They are sold by weight in cellophane packets wherever Oriental foods are available.

WHAT TO DRINK

Try a slightly sweet light German wine such as a Riesling *Kabinett* from the Moselle or the Rhine. Or serve a Chinese or Japanese beer.

SHOPPING LIST AND STAPLES

1½ pounds rare roast beef, thinly sliced
¼ pound Westphalian or other smoked ham, sliced
¼ pound snow peas
Small red bell pepper

Small bunch celery
¼ pound fresh mung bean sprouts
3 bunches scallions
1-inch piece fresh ginger
2 cloves garlic
1 bunch coriander
2 eggs
1 pound fresh Chinese egg vermicelli, or ½ pound dried vermicelli
2 tablespoons peanut oil
7 tablespoons Oriental sesame oil
1 tablespoon rice or white wine vinegar
2 tablespoons Chinese black vinegar or white wine vinegar
2 tablespoons light soy sauce
1 ounce dried Chinese black mushrooms
2½-ounce jar sesame seeds
1 tablespoon plus 2 teaspoons sugar
Salt

UTENSILS

Stockpot
Medium-size skillet
Small heavy-gauge skillet
Medium-size saucepan

3 small bowls
Colander
Large strainer
Measuring cups and spoons
Chef's knife
Paring knife
2 wooden spoons
Metal spatula
Small whisk
Kitchen scissors

START-TO-FINISH STEPS

1. Follow vermicelli salad recipe steps 1 through 10.
2. Follow beef salad recipe steps 1 through 8.
3. Follow vermicelli salad recipe steps 11 through 13.
4. Follow beef salad recipe step 9 and serve with vermicelli salad.

RECIPES

Chinese Egg Vermicelli with Vegetables and Ham

10 dried Chinese black mushrooms (about 1 ounce total weight)

1 pound fresh Chinese egg vermicelli, or ½ pound dried
  vermicelli
Salt
¼ pound snow peas
¼ pound Westphalian or other smoked ham, sliced
1 bunch coriander
1 cup fresh mung bean sprouts
1 tablespoon peanut oil
2 eggs
2 teaspoons sugar
2 tablespoons Chinese black vinegar or white wine
  vinegar
1 tablespoon light soy sauce
6 tablespoons Oriental sesame oil

1. For mushrooms, bring 1 cup water to a boil in tea kettle. For vermicelli, combine 4 quarts water and 1 tablespoon salt in stockpot and bring to a boil over high heat.
2. In small bowl, combine dried mushrooms with 1 cup boiling water and set aside.
3. For snow peas, bring 1 quart water and 1 tablespoon salt to a boil in medium-size saucepan over high heat.
4. Meanwhile, cut ham into 2-inch-long by ¼-inch-wide strips; set aside.
5. Plunge snow peas into boiling water in saucepan and blanch 30 seconds. Turn into colander and refresh under cold running water; drain. Dry and set aside.
6. Wash and dry coriander. Trim off stems and discard. Coarsely chop coriander; set aside.
7. Place sprouts in colander, rinse under cold running water, and drain. Dry sprouts and set aside.
8. Add vermicelli to boiling water in stockpot and cook 1 minute for fresh, or according to package instructions for dried. Transfer vermicelli to large strainer and refresh under cold running water; set aside to drain.
9. In medium-size skillet, heat peanut oil over medium-high heat.
10. Meanwhile, using fork, beat eggs in small bowl until blended. Add to skillet and cook about 3 minutes per side, or until firm. Carefully slip omelet out onto plate in one piece; set aside. Rinse and dry bowl.
11. Drain mushrooms and rinse under cold water. Using kitchen scissors, cut off stems and discard. Cut mushrooms into ¼-inch-wide strips. Cut omelet into ½-inch-wide strips; set aside.
12. For dressing, combine sugar, vinegar, and soy sauce in small bowl. Whisking vigorously, gradually add sesame oil and stir until blended.
13. In large serving bowl or on platter, combine vermicelli, snow peas, mushrooms, ham, sprouts, half the coriander, and toss to combine. Pour dressing over salad and toss until evenly coated. Arrange omelet strips around salad and sprinkle with remaining coriander.

Cold Beef Salad with Ginger Dressing

2 tablespoons sesame seeds
2 cloves garlic
1-inch piece fresh ginger

1 tablespoon sugar
1 tablespoon rice or white wine vinegar
1 tablespoon light soy sauce
1 tablespoon Oriental sesame oil
1 tablespoon peanut oil
1½ pounds rare roast beef, thinly sliced
Small red bell pepper
1 tablespoon salt
3 bunches scallions
2 stalks celery

1. In small heavy-gauge skillet, toast sesame seeds over medium heat, stirring constantly to prevent scorching, 2 minutes, or until lightly browned and fragrant. Transfer to plate and set aside to cool.
2. Peel and mince garlic. Peel and mince enough ginger to measure 2 teaspoons.
3. Combine garlic, ginger, sugar, vinegar, and soy sauce in small bowl. Whisking continuously, gradually add sesame and peanut oil and stir until blended; set aside.
4. Cut roast beef into ¼-inch-wide strips. You should have about 4 cups. Set aside.
5. Wash and dry red bell pepper. Halve, core, and seed pepper. Cut into ¼-inch-wide strips; set aside.
6. Combine 1 quart water with salt in medium-size saucepan and bring to a boil over high heat.
7. Meanwhile, trim off ends from scallions and celery and discard. Cut scallions into 3-inch-long pieces and cut celery on diagonal into ⅛-inch-thick slices. Add celery to boiling water and blanch 2 minutes. Then add scallions and blanch another 15 seconds. Transfer vegetables to colander and refresh under cold running water; drain. Pat dry with paper towels.
8. In shallow serving bowl or on platter, combine beef, red bell pepper, celery, and scallions, and toss to combine.
9. Whisk dressing to recombine. Pour dressing over salad and toss until evenly coated. Sprinkle with toasted sesame seeds and serve.

———————

ADDED TOUCH

For this simple dessert, select berries that are bright red and plump, with no tinges of white or green.

Sweet-and-Sour Strawberries

2 pints strawberries
2 tablespoons granulated sugar
1 tablespoon raspberry vinegar
1 cup sour cream
2 tablespoons brown sugar

1. Gently rinse strawberries under cold running water and dry. Hull berries and halve lengthwise.
2. Combine granulated sugar and vinegar in large bowl and stir with fork until blended. Add berries and toss until evenly coated. Set aside for at least 30 minutes.
3. Divide berries among 4 bowls and top each serving with a heaping tablespoon of sour cream. Sprinkle with brown sugar and serve.

Meat and Vegetable Salad
Creole-style Potato Salad with Sausage
Romaine Lettuce and Tomatoes with Blue Cheese and Anchovy Dressing

Creole-style potatoes and sausage go well with a light meat and vegetable salad and with romaine lettuce and tomatoes.

This three-salad menu is good throughout the year and can be altered to use what you have on hand. For instance, in the cold meat salad you can use lean pork or ham, chicken, or dark-meat turkey. If asparagus is not in season, you can use broccoli, green beans, or cauliflower instead. If you prefer a vegetarian salad, omit the meat.

The hot potato salad is very spicy; for a milder version, reduce the amount of hot pepper sauce and Cayenne. The Louisiana *andouille* sausage used in this recipe imparts a distinctive smoky flavor. Unlike French *andouille,* this American version is made with pork meat rather than intestines. It is highly seasoned with garlic and Cayenne pepper before being smoked. You can substitute Polish *kielbasa* or Portuguese *linguiça* sausages, but these lack the intense flavor of *andouille.* The salad dressing contains Creole mustard, a pungent coarse-grained brown mustard that sometimes includes horseradish. Look for it in specialty food shops.

WHAT TO DRINK

A robust white wine such as an Alsatian Sylvaner or Pinot Blanc or an earthy red Côtes du Rhône or California Zinfandel would go nicely with the flavors of these dishes.

SHOPPING LIST AND STAPLES

½ pound cooked pork, chicken, or turkey
½ pound Louisiana andouille, linguiça, or kielbasa
   sausage
2 pounds small red boiling potatoes
1 pound green beans
1 head romaine lettuce
2 medium-size tomatoes
1 pint cherry tomatoes
Small red onion
1 bunch scallions
2 cloves garlic
Small bunch parsley
2 lemons
Large egg
¼ pound blue cheese
1¼ cups olive oil
½ cup peanut oil
6 tablespoons cider vinegar
2 tablespoons red wine vinegar
3 tablespoons Dijon mustard, approximately
1 tablespoon Creole mustard (optional)
Hot pepper sauce
2½-ounce tin anchovy fillets
3½-ounce can sliced almonds
1 tablespoon dried oregano
¼ teaspoon Cayenne pepper
Salt and freshly ground black pepper

UTENSILS

Food processor or blender
Medium-size skillet
Medium-size saucepan with cover
Cookie sheet
Large bowl
Salad spinner (optional)
Colander
Measuring cups and spoons
Chef's knife
Paring knife
2 wooden spoons
Slotted spoon
Rubber spatula
Whisk
Juicer

START-TO-FINISH STEPS

1. Wash scallions and dry with paper towels. Trim off ends and discard. Mince enough scallions to measure ½ cup for potato salad recipe and coarsely chop enough to measure ¼ cup for meat and vegetable salad recipe; set aside.
2. Follow potato salad recipe steps 1 through 3.
3. While potatoes are cooking, follow meat and vegetable salad recipe steps 1 through 10.
4. Follow potato salad recipe step 4 and romaine salad recipe steps 1 through 3.
5. Follow potato salad recipe steps 5 through 10.
6. Follow meat and vegetable salad recipe steps 11 and 12, and rinse and dry food processor or blender.
7. Follow romaine salad recipe steps 4 through 6.
8. Follow potato salad recipe steps 11 and 12, and serve with meat and vegetable salad and romaine salad.

RECIPES

Meat and Vegetable Salad

Salt
1 pound green beans
½ pint cherry tomatoes
¼ cup sliced almonds
½ pound cooked pork, chicken, or turkey
2 lemons
2 teaspoons Dijon mustard
Large egg
½ cup peanut oil
½ cup olive oil
Freshly ground black pepper
¼ cup coarsely chopped scallions

1. Preheat oven to 350 degrees.
2. Combine 2 quarts water and 2 tablespoons salt in medium-size saucepan and bring to a boil over high heat.
3. Meanwhile, trim off ends of beans and discard. Cut beans in half.
4. Wash, dry, and halve cherry tomatoes; set aside.
5. Add beans to boiling water and cook 3 to 5 minutes, or until crisp-tender.
6. While beans are cooking, arrange almonds on cookie sheet in a single layer and place in oven, shaking pan occasionally to prevent scorching, 5 to 8 minutes, or until lightly toasted.
7. Cut meat into ½-inch dice to measure 2 cups; set aside.

8. Turn beans into colander and refresh under cold running water; set aside to drain.

9. Squeeze enough lemon juice to measure ¼ cup.

10. Remove almonds from oven and set aside to cool.

11. For dressing, combine lemon juice, mustard, and egg in food processor or blender and process just until blended. With machine running, gradually add peanut oil until mixture begins to thicken. Then add remaining peanut oil and olive oil in a slow, steady stream and process until thick and creamy. Add salt and pepper to taste.

12. Combine meat, beans, tomatoes, and scallions, and half the toasted almonds in large serving bowl. Add just enough dressing to bind salad and toss to combine. Reserve remaining dressing for another use. Sprinkle salad with remaining almonds and set aside until ready to serve.

Creole-style Potato Salad with Sausage

Salt
2 pounds small red boiling potatoes
Small red onion
½ cup minced scallions
¼ cup minced parsley
6 tablespoons cider vinegar
4 leaves romaine lettuce (optional)
6 tablespoons olive oil
½ pound Louisiana andouille, linguiça, or kielbasa
    sausage
1 clove garlic, minced
1 tablespoon Creole or Dijon mustard
¼ teaspoon Cayenne pepper
½ teaspoon freshly ground black pepper
Hot pepper sauce

1. In medium-size saucepan, bring 2 quarts water, 1 tablespoon salt, and potatoes to a boil over high heat.

2. While water is coming to a boil, peel and mince enough red onion to measure ½ cup; set aside.

3. When water comes to a boil, partially cover pot, reduce heat to medium-high, and cook potatoes 20 to 30 minutes, or until they can be pierced easily with tip of sharp knife.

4. When potatoes are cooked, turn into colander to drain and set aside to cool.

5. When potatoes are cool enough to handle, cut each in half and then into ¼-inch-thick slices.

6. Combine potatoes, onion, scallions, and parsley in large bowl and sprinkle with 3 tablespoons cider vinegar.

7. Line serving platter with romaine, if using.

8. Heat olive oil in medium-size skillet over medium heat.

9. Coarsely chop sausage. Add sausage to skillet and sauté, stirring, 3 minutes, or just until it begins to brown.

10. Remove pan from heat and, with slotted spoon, transfer sausage to paper towels to drain. Add sausage to vegetables.

11. To fat remaining in pan, add garlic, mustard, Cayenne, remaining 3 tablespoons vinegar, pepper, and hot pepper sauce to taste and bring to a boil, whisking continuously, over medium-high heat.

12. Pour hot vinaigrette over salad and toss gently to combine. Turn out onto platter and serve immediately.

Romaine Lettuce and Tomatoes with Blue Cheese and Anchovy Dressing

1 head romaine lettuce
2 medium-size tomatoes
¼ pound blue cheese
1 clove garlic, peeled
4 anchovy fillets
1 tablespoon Dijon mustard
2 tablespoons red wine vinegar
1 tablespoon dried oregano
6 tablespoons olive oil

1. Wash and dry lettuce. Tear leaves into quarters. Wrap in paper towels and refrigerate until ready to serve.

2. Wash and dry tomatoes. Core each tomato and cut into wedges; set aside.

3. Crumble enough cheese into small pieces to measure ¼ cup; set aside.

4. For dressing, combine garlic, anchovy fillets, mustard, vinegar, and oregano in food processor or blender and process just until paste-like.

5. With machine running, add olive oil in a slow, steady stream and process until mixture is creamy.

6. In large salad bowl, combine romaine and tomato wedges. Pour dressing over salad and toss until evenly coated. Sprinkle with cheese and set aside until ready to serve.

LEFTOVER SUGGESTION

Reheat leftover Creole potato salad by sautéing it briefly until the potatoes and onions turn crisp and brown. When served with a tossed green salad, it makes a substantial luncheon.

Jane Uetz

When planning her meals, whether formal or informal, Jane Uetz likes to inject a surprise element that generally elicits comments from her guests. Often it is an unusual combination of ingredients. For example, in her rich Menu 1 salad, adapted from a dish she once sampled in the Spanish Pavilion restaurant at the New York World's Fair, she arranges sliced fruits around chunks of fresh lobster dressed with an unusual tarragon- and sherry-flavored mayonnaise. The salad is preceded by consommé Madrilène, a tomato soup that may be served hot or chilled, and whole-wheat muffins with chives.

The height-of-summer salad in Menu 3 combines cherry tomatoes and melon balls—an unexpected tart-sweet mix—with slices of Black Forest ham. The cook also offers hard-boiled eggs stuffed with tapénade—a paste of capers, anchovies, garlic, egg yolks, and lemon juice. The word tapénade derives from the Provençal *tapéno,* meaning capers, a traditional ingredient in this popular spread.

For the warm salad of Menu 2, Jane Uetz pairs lentils (often bland when served alone) and highly spiced Spanish *chorizo* sausage, and binds them with a tangy vinaigrette. A creamy vegetable soup made from cauliflower, carrots, onion, and celery tempers the sausage, and a second salad of green beans and red pepper strips adds color and texture.

Fresh flowers set a festive tone for this sumptuous meal. Garnish each mug of consommé with a slice of lemon and a sprig of coriander if you like, and offer a basket of muffins hot from the oven. The lobster and fruit salad, with its creamy mayonnaise dressing, is arranged on a bed of red leaf lettuce.

Consommé Madrilène
Lobster and Fruit Salad with Tarragon-Sherry Mayonnaise
Whole-Wheat Muffins with Chives

The North American lobster, prized for its rich meat, turns any meal into a feast. Buy live lobsters that are very active in the tank. You will need a lobster steamer or a stockpot large enough to accommodate two lobsters. Once the salted water boils, rinse the lobsters briefly under cold water, then plunge them into the pot. To test for doneness, remove each lobster from the cooking water with tongs and pull off one small leg; the lobster is fully cooked when the leg comes off readily.

WHAT TO DRINK

A full-bodied white wine is nice with this meal. Good choices would be a California Chardonnay or a white Burgundy such as Mâcon or Saint-Véran.

SHOPPING LIST AND STAPLES

Two 2- to 2¼-pound live lobsters, or two 8-ounce packages frozen lobster tails
2 pounds very ripe fresh tomatoes, or 32-ounce can plum tomatoes
1 head red leaf lettuce
Medium-size red bell pepper
Small bunch fresh chives
Small bunch fresh coriander
Small bunch fresh tarragon, or ½ teaspoon dried
2 lemons
1 orange
1 ripe pear
1 large banana
4 cups chicken stock, preferably homemade (see page 9), or canned
1 cup milk
½ pint heavy cream
¼ cup shortening (not oil)
⅓ cup mayonnaise, preferably homemade (see page 12)
3 tablespoons ketchup
1 cup all-purpose flour
1 cup whole-wheat flour
3 teaspoons baking powder
Salt
2 tablespoons dry sherry

UTENSILS

Food processor or blender
Large stockpot with cover
Medium-size saucepan with cover
Large bowl
Medium-size bowl
3 small bowls
12-cup muffin pan
Colander
Measuring cups and spoons
Chef's knife
Paring knife
Ladle
Rubber spatula
Nutcracker
Pastry blender (optional)
Metal tongs

START-TO-FINISH STEPS

1. Wash coriander, chives, and fresh tarragon if using, and dry with paper towels. Reserve 4 sprigs coriander for garnish, if desired, and chop enough of remainder to measure 1 tablespoon for consommé recipe. Snip enough chives to measure ¼ cup for muffin recipe. Chop enough tarragon to measure 1 teaspoon for salad recipe. Juice 1½ lemons for salad recipe, and cut 4 slices from remaining lemon half for consommé garnish, if desired.
2. Follow salad recipe steps 1 through 7.
3. While lobster is cooling, follow consommé recipe steps 1 through 4.
4. Follow salad recipe steps 8 and 9.
5. Follow muffin recipe steps 1 through 6.
6. Follow consommé recipe steps 5 through 7.
7. Follow muffin recipe step 7, and serve with consommé as first course.
8. Follow salad recipe steps 10 and 11 and serve.

RECIPES

Consommé Madrilène

2 pounds very ripe fresh tomatoes, or 32-ounce can plum tomatoes
1 tablespoon chopped fresh coriander, plus 4 sprigs for garnish (optional)
4 cups chicken stock
4 lemon slices for garnish (optional)

1. If using fresh tomatoes, bring 2 quarts of water to a boil

in medium-size saucepan over high heat.

2. Plunge tomatoes into boiling water and blanch 30 seconds. Turn tomatoes into colander and refresh under cold water. Peel, quarter, and remove seeds. If using canned tomatoes, drain, quarter, and remove seeds.

3. In medium-size saucepan, combine tomatoes, chopped coriander, and stock, and bring to a boil over high heat. Reduce heat to medium, cover pan, and simmer 15 minutes.

4. Remove soup from heat, uncover pan and set aside to cool.

5. Transfer soup to food processor or blender and purée. If using processor, purée soup in batches.

6. Return soup to saucepan and heat through over medium heat.

7. Divide soup among 4 mugs or bowls and garnish each serving with a slice of lemon and a sprig of coriander, if desired.

Lobster and Fruit Salad with Tarragon-Sherry Mayonnaise

Salt
⅓ cup mayonnaise
3 tablespoons heavy cream
3 tablespoons ketchup
2 tablespoons dry sherry
1 teaspoon chopped fresh tarragon, or ½ teaspoon dried
Two 2- to 2¼-pound lobsters, or two 8-ounce packages frozen lobster tails, cooked according to package directions
Medium-size red bell pepper
1 orange
Juice of 1½ lemons
1 ripe pear
1 head red leaf lettuce
1 large banana

1. In large stockpot, bring 5 cups salted water to a boil over high heat.

2. Meanwhile, combine mayonnaise, heavy cream, ketchup, sherry, and tarragon in small bowl, stirring until well blended. Cover dressing with plastic wrap and set aside.

3. Add lobsters to boiling water head first, cover pot, and cook over high heat 15 minutes.

4. Meanwhile, wash bell pepper and dry with paper towel. Halve, core, and seed pepper. Cut into ¼-inch-wide strips; set aside.

5. Peel orange, removing as much white pith as possible. Cut crosswise into ¼-inch-thick rounds; set aside.

6. In small bowl, combine 2 tablespoons lemon juice and 2 cups cold water. Halve pear and cut lengthwise into ¼-inch-thick slices. Add pear slices to lemon water to prevent discoloration; set aside.

7. With tongs, transfer lobsters to colander and set aside to cool.

8. Wash lettuce and dry with paper towels. Remove and discard any bruised or discolored leaves. Line serving platter with lettuce, cover with plastic wrap, and refrigerate until ready to serve.

9. When lobsters are completely cool, remove meat from shells, using nutcracker to crack claws. Discard shells. Cut meat into bite-size pieces and place in large bowl. You should have about 4 cups meat.

10. Peel banana and cut on diagonal into 1½-inch slices. Place banana in small bowl and sprinkle with remaining lemon juice. Toss slices to coat evenly.

11. Spoon lobster into center of lettuce-lined platter and arrange fruit slices and pepper strips around it. Drizzle some mayonnaise over lobster and serve remaining mayonnaise on the side.

Whole-Wheat Muffins with Chives

1 cup all-purpose flour
1 cup whole-wheat flour
3 teaspoons baking powder
1 teaspoon salt
¼ cup shortening (not oil)
1 cup milk
¼ cup snipped chives

1. Preheat oven to 450 degrees.

2. Grease 12-cup muffin pan.

3. In medium-size bowl, combine all-purpose and whole-wheat flour, baking powder, and salt, and stir with fork to blend.

4. Cut in shortening with pastry blender or 2 knives until mixture resembles coarse cornmeal.

5. With your fist, make a well in center of flour mixture. Add milk and chives, and, using a fork, stir just enough to moisten dry ingredients.

6. Fill each cup of muffin pan half full with batter and bake 12 to 15 minutes, or until muffins are golden.

7. Transfer muffins to napkin-lined basket and serve hot.

ADDED TOUCH

Serve this spread of pungent Roquefort cheese, Armagnac, and orange-flavored liqueur at room temperature for easier spreading and fuller flavor.

Armagnac Cheese Spread

¼ pound Roquefort cheese
¼ pound cream cheese
1 stick unsalted butter
2 tablespoons Armagnac
1½ teaspoons orange liqueur, such as Grand Marnier or Cointreau
¼ cup chopped walnuts
Water biscuits or other unsalted crackers

1. Allow cheeses and butter to soften at room temperature.

2. Using electric mixer, blend cheeses with butter in medium-size bowl until creamy.

3. Still beating, gradually add Armagnac and orange liqueur, and beat until mixture is smooth.

4. Stir in walnuts. Serve the spread with crisp crackers.

Cream of Winter Vegetable Soup
Warm Lentil and Sausage Salad
Green Beans and Red Pepper Strips in Mustard Vinaigrette

The main-course salad features lentils and *chorizo* sausage. The lentils should be washed before use to remove any tiny pebbles, but they do not require presoaking. Spanish *chorizo* is a pork sausage highly spiced with Cayenne and garlic. Some *chorizos* are sold fresh, but most are dried and smoked. Use the dried type for this recipe. *Chorizo* is available in some supermarkets and at stores selling Hispanic foods. You can substitute a hard salami, such as Genoa, or pepperoni, but because they are even more garlicky than *chorizo*, eliminate the garlic from the dressing.

For a filling dinner on a cold winter's night, serve steaming bowls of vegetable soup topped with sour cream and parsley, lentil and sausage salad with a red-wine vinegar dressing, and green beans with red pepper strips.

WHAT TO DRINK

Serve your guests a full-flavored Zinfandel, a shipper's Châteauneuf-du-Pape, or an Italian Dolcetto with these dishes. Or you can follow the cook's suggestion for an amber English beer or ale.

SHOPPING LIST AND STAPLES

½ pound chorizo or other dried hot sausage
1 pound green beans
Small head cauliflower (about 1 pound)
2 medium-size yellow or white onions (about 1 pound total weight)
Small red onion
2 medium-size carrots

Small bunch celery
Large red bell pepper
1 bunch watercress
1 clove garlic
Small bunch parsley
1 lemon
4 cups chicken stock, preferably homemade (see page 9), or canned
1 cup milk
½ pint sour cream (optional)
3 tablespoons unsalted butter
1 cup vegetable oil, approximately
2 tablespoons red wine vinegar
1½ tablespoons cider vinegar
1 teaspoon balsamic vinegar
2 teaspoons Pommery or other coarse-grained mustard
¼ teaspoon hot pepper sauce
1 cup brown lentils
¼ cup flour
¼ teaspoon sugar
½ teaspoon dried tarragon
¼ teaspoon ground cumin
1½ bay leaves
Salt
Freshly ground pepper
¼ teaspoon whole black peppercorns

UTENSILS

Food processor or blender
Small nonstick skillet
2 large saucepans with covers
Medium-size saucepan with cover
Small saucepan
Large bowl
Medium-size bowl
2 small bowls
Colander or large strainer
Measuring cups and spoons
Chef's knife
Paring knife
Wooden spoon
Slotted spoon
Ladle
Whisk
Vegetable peeler
Juicer
Cheesecloth

START-TO-FINISH STEPS

1. Peel and chop enough onion to measure ½ cup each for soup and salad recipes. Wash and dry parsley; mince

enough to measure ¼ cup each for salad and soup recipes.
2. Follow soup recipe steps 1 through 6.
3. While soup is simmering, follow salad recipe steps 1 through 4 and green beans recipe steps 1 through 7.
4. Follow salad recipe step 5 and soup recipe step 7.
5. Follow salad recipe steps 6 through 8.
6. Follow soup recipe steps 8 through 12.
7. Follow salad recipe step 9, soup recipe step 13, and serve with green beans.

RECIPES

Cream of Winter Vegetable Soup

Small head cauliflower (about 1 pound)
2 medium-size carrots
2 stalks celery
3 tablespoons unsalted butter
½ cup chopped yellow or white onion
¼ teaspoon whole black peppercorns
½ teaspoon dried tarragon
½ bay leaf
4 cups chicken stock
¼ cup flour
1 cup milk
Salt and freshly ground pepper
½ cup sour cream (optional)
¼ cup minced parsley

1. Rinse cauliflower. Cut into florets; set aside.
2. Peel carrots. Cut crosswise into 1-inch-long pieces.
3. Wash celery and chop enough to measure ¾ cup.
4. In large saucepan, heat 1 tablespoon butter over medium heat. Add onion and sauté, stirring occasionally, 5 minutes, or until onion is soft and translucent.
5. Meanwhile, prepare *bouquet garni* by making a small pouch from a double thickness of cheesecloth. Place peppercorns, tarragon, and ½ bay leaf in pouch, and tie securely with kitchen string.
6. Add vegetables, 2 cups stock, and *bouquet garni* to saucepan, and bring to a boil over high heat. Reduce heat to medium-low, cover pan, and simmer 30 minutes.
7. Remove *bouquet garni* and discard. Set pan of vegetables aside to cool slightly.
8. Transfer vegetables to food processor, or to a blender if you want a smoother texture, and purée. Return purée to saucepan; set aside.
9. In small saucepan, melt remaining 2 tablespoons butter over medium-low heat. Whisk in flour and cook 1 minute.
10. Remove pan from heat. Whisking continuously, add milk in a slow, steady stream and stir until blended. Return pan to medium-high heat and bring to a boil.
11. Whisking continuously, add milk mixture to vegetable purée and stir until blended. Whisk in remaining stock.
12. Place soup over high heat and bring to a boil. Add salt and pepper to taste.
13. Divide soup among 4 bowls and garnish with sour cream and parsley, if desired.

Warm Lentil and Sausage Salad

½ pound chorizo or other dried hot sausage
1 cup brown lentils
½ cup chopped yellow or white onion
1 teaspoon salt
1 bay leaf
1 bunch watercress
Small red onion for garnish
¼ teaspoon minced garlic
2 tablespoons lemon juice
½ cup vegetable oil
2 tablespoons red wine vinegar
¼ teaspoon ground cumin
¼ teaspoon hot pepper sauce
¼ cup minced parsley

1. Remove casing from chorizo and cut sausage into 1½-inch-long by ½-inch-wide strips. In small nonstick skillet, sauté chorizo about 5 minutes, or until lightly browned.
2. Rinse lentils in colander or large strainer; drain.
3. Transfer chorizo to paper towels to drain.
4. In large saucepan, combine lentils, onion, salt, bay leaf, and 1 quart cold water, and bring to a boil over high heat. Reduce heat to medium, cover pan, and simmer gently 15 to 17 minutes, or until lentils are tender.
5. Drain lentils; discard bay leaf. Cover pan.
6. Wash and dry watercress. Trim stems and discard.
7. Peel red onion and cut into ⅛-inch-thick slices.
8. For dressing, in small bowl, combine garlic, lemon juice, and remaining ingredients except parsley, and stir with fork until blended; set aside.
9. Just before serving, combine lentils and sausage in large bowl. Pour dressing over salad and toss. Divide salad among 4 dinner plates and sprinkle with parsley. Garnish with watercress and red onion slices, and serve.

Green Beans and Red Pepper Strips in Mustard Vinaigrette

1 pound green beans
¼ teaspoon salt
Large red bell pepper
¼ teaspoon sugar
1 teaspoon balsamic vinegar
1½ tablespoons cider vinegar
2 teaspoons Pommery or other coarse-grained mustard
⅓ cup vegetable oil

1. Bring 2 cups of water to a boil in medium-size saucepan.
2. In colander, rinse beans in cold water and trim ends.
3. Add salt and beans to boiling water, cover pan, and cook 3 to 5 minutes, or just until beans are crisp-tender.
4. Wash and dry red pepper. Core, halve, and seed pepper. Cut lengthwise into ¼-inch-wide strips.
5. For vinaigrette, combine sugar and remaining ingredients in small bowl and stir with fork until blended.
6. Turn beans into colander and refresh under cold water.
7. In medium-size serving bowl, combine beans and pepper strips. Pour vinaigrette over vegetables and toss.

Stuffed Eggs Tapénade
Cherry Tomato and Melon Salad with Smoked Ham
Fried Goat Cheese with Garlic Bread

Melon balls with cherry tomatoes and ham, goat cheese on garlic bread, and stuffed eggs are a colorful company meal.

Two types of melon and smoked ham make a delectable combination. To get a good cantaloupe, select one with a smooth depression at the stem end, indicating the melon was nearly ripe when picked; it will only need to stand a few days at room temperature to soften. When ripe, the cantaloupe will emit a distinctive aroma. Choose a honeydew with a yellowish skin color and slightly waxy or oily-looking surface. Sniff the stem end; a vine-ripened honeydew will have a sweet fragrance. A honeydew with hard, green-tinged skin was picked too early and will never achieve the full flavor of a vine-ripened melon. You can keep a honeydew at room temperature for a few days.

If you like, try other melons such as Casaba, Santa Claus, or Crenshaw. Although the salad is best with fresh melon balls, you can use the frozen type as a winter substitute. If you cannot buy Black Forest or Westphalian ham, substitute smoked turkey or salami.

For the fried goat cheese, use a log-shaped Montrachet without an ash coating. This French import is soft, moist, and has only a touch of the "goatiness" associated with many goat cheeses. Montrachet is sold at most cheese or specialty food stores. It slices and fries best when very cold, so place it in the freezer for at least five minutes to firm it.

WHAT TO DRINK

This menu, with its bold flavors, demands a crisp white wine or a light red one. For a white, choose Sancerre, Pouilly-Fumé, or Sauvignon Blanc; for a red, try a young Zinfandel or Gamay Beaujolais.

SHOPPING LIST AND STAPLES

½ pound thinly sliced smoked ham, such as Black
   Forest or Westphalian
1 head red leaf lettuce
1 pint cherry tomatoes
2 cloves garlic
Small bunch fresh parsley
Small bunch fresh basil, or ½ to 1 teaspoon dried
Small bunch fresh chives, or 2-ounce container
   frozen
1 lemon
Small cantaloupe
Small honeydew or other melon
4 large eggs
4 tablespoons unsalted butter, approximately
½-pound log Montrachet cheese
½ cup olive oil, approximately
1 tablespoon white wine vinegar
1 teaspoon Dijon mustard
2-ounce jar capers
2-ounce tin anchovy fillets, or 1 tablespoon anchovy
   paste
1 baguette (¼-pound loaf)
2 slices home-style white bread

¼ teaspoon paprika
Salt

UTENSILS

Food processor or blender
Medium-size skillet
Small saucepan with cover
Heatproof platter
Large bowl
Medium-size bowl
Small bowl
9-inch pie pan or shallow dish
Salad spinner (optional)
Measuring cups and spoons
Chef's knife
Bread knife
2 wooden spoons
Slotted spatula
Melon baller

START-TO-FINISH STEPS

One hour ahead: Set eggs out to reach room temperature.

1. Peel and mince garlic for eggs recipe and cheese recipe. Wash parsley, and fresh herbs if using, and dry with paper towels. Reserve 8 sprigs of parsley for garnish, if using, for eggs recipe. Trim stems and mince enough parsley to measure 1 tablespoon for eggs recipe. Chop enough basil and snip enough chives to measure 1 tablespoon each for salad recipe. Squeeze enough lemon juice to measure 1 teaspoon for eggs recipe and 2 tablespoons for salad recipe.
2. Follow eggs recipe steps 1 and 2, and salad recipe steps 1 through 4.
3. Follow eggs recipe step 3 and cheese recipe steps 1 through 4.
4. Follow eggs recipe steps 4 through 7.
5. Follow salad recipe steps 5 and 6, cheese recipe steps 5 through 9, and serve with eggs.

RECIPES

Stuffed Eggs Tapénade

4 large eggs, at room temperature
2-ounce jar capers
2-ounce tin anchovy fillets, or 1 tablespoon
   anchovy paste
1 clove garlic, minced
1 tablespoon minced parsley, plus 8 sprigs for
   garnish (optional)
1 teaspoon Dijon mustard
1 teaspoon lemon juice
1 tablespoon white wine vinegar
1 tablespoon olive oil

1. Place eggs in small saucepan and add enough cold water to cover by at least 1 inch. Cover pan and bring water to a rapid boil over high heat.

2. When water reaches a rapid boil, turn off heat and let eggs sit on stove 15 minutes.

3. Fill medium-size bowl half full with cold water. Transfer eggs to cold water and set aside to cool.

4. Drain 1 teaspoon capers and mince. If using anchovy fillets, drain 3 fillets and mince.

5. In small bowl, combine capers, anchovies, garlic, minced parsley, mustard, lemon juice, vinegar, and oil, and stir with fork until blended.

6. Peel hard-boiled eggs and halve lengthwise. Add yolks to bowl and mash ingredients together with fork to form a smooth tapénade paste.

7. Fill whites with tapénade and divide stuffed eggs among 4 salad plates. Garnish plates with parsley sprigs, if desired.

Cherry Tomato and Melon Salad with Smoked Ham

1 pint cherry tomatoes
Small cantaloupe
Small honeydew or other melon
⅓ cup olive oil
2 tablespoons lemon juice
¼ teaspoon salt
1 to 2 tablespoons chopped fresh basil, or ½ to 1 teaspoon dried
1 to 2 tablespoons snipped fresh or frozen chives
1 head red leaf lettuce
½ pound thinly sliced smoked ham, such as Black Forest or Westphalian

1. Wash tomatoes and dry with paper towels. Halve tomatoes; set aside.

2. Halve cantaloupe and small honeydew melons; remove and discard seeds. Using large end of melon baller, carefully scoop out enough flesh to measure about 6 cups of melon balls.

3. In large bowl, combine oil, lemon juice, salt, and 1 to 2 tablespoons each of fresh basil and chives, depending on sweetness of melons.

4. Add melon balls and tomato halves to dressing in bowl; toss until evenly coated. Cover bowl and let stand 30 minutes at room temperature.

5. Wash lettuce and dry in salad spinner or with paper towels. Remove and discard any bruised or discolored leaves. Divide lettuce among 4 large plates and top with melon and tomatoes.

6. Roll up each slice of ham; arrange slices around salad and serve.

Fried Goat Cheese with Garlic Bread

2 slices home-style white bread
¼ teaspoon paprika
½-pound log Montrachet cheese, well chilled
4 tablespoons unsalted butter, approximately
1 tablespoon olive oil
1 clove garlic, minced
1 baguette (¼-pound loaf)

1. Preheat oven to 200 degrees.

2. Trim crusts from white bread and discard; chop bread coarsely. Using food processor or blender, process bread into crumbs. You should have about ½ cup.

3. In pie pan or shallow dish, combine bread crumbs and paprika.

4. Place cheese in freezer to chill at least 5 minutes.

5. Cut well-chilled cheese into eight ½-inch-thick slices. Dip each cheese slice in bread crumbs and press to help crumbs adhere.

6. In medium-size skillet, heat 2 tablespoons butter over medium-high heat. When butter stops foaming, add all of the cheese slices and fry 1 minute per side, or until lightly browned and cheese is warm and soft. Using slotted spatula, transfer cheese to heatproof platter and keep warm in oven.

7. Reduce heat under skillet to medium-low. Add remaining butter, olive oil, and garlic to skillet and sauté 1 minute.

8. Meanwhile, cut baguette on diagonal into eight ½-inch-thick slices. Add bread slices to skillet and sauté, adding more butter, if necessary, 1 minute per side, or until lightly browned.

9. Transfer bread slices to serving platter and top with cheese.

ADDED TOUCH

When melting the chocolate, be sure to include the shortening, or the chocolate will be too thick to properly coat the sherbet balls. The cook suggests using a Jaffa orange, an Israeli variety, for the garnish, but any other type of orange will do.

Frosted Sherbet Balls

1 quart orange sherbet
4 squares semi-sweet chocolate
2 tablespoons shortening (not oil)
1 Jaffa or other orange for garnish (optional)
4 fresh mint sprigs for garnish (optional)

1. Line a metal freezer tray with waxed paper or aluminum foil.

2. Using ice cream scoop, scoop sherbet into 8 balls and place on tray. Keep chilled in freezer.

3. Combine chocolate and shortening in top of double boiler and place over hot water, stirring occasionally, until chocolate melts.

4. Remove top of double boiler from hot water and set chocolate aside to cool slightly, about 3 minutes.

5. Remove sherbet balls from freezer. Drizzle each one with chocolate until coated and return to freezer.

6. Place 4 dessert plates in freezer to chill.

7. With sharp paring knife, peel orange, if using, removing as much white pith as possible. Segment orange.

8. Wash mint sprigs, if using, and dry with paper towel.

9. Divide sherbet balls among chilled dessert plates and garnish each serving with orange sections and a mint sprig, if desired.

Mary Carroll Dremann

Like many of her fellow Californians, Mary Carroll Dremann loves to create bountiful salads using the local farm-fresh produce available on the West Coast year round. To the delight of her guests, she often goes beyond the standard salad makings and incorporates ethnic ingredients to achieve intriguing flavor combinations. For an exciting visual presentation, she likes to cut fruits and vegetables into various shapes. And to emphasize rather than obscure the natural flavor of each ingredient, she dresses the salads lightly.

The Oriental salad of Menu 1 has a sesame oil, *tamari,* and rice vinegar dressing flavored with ginger, coriander, and honey, which is also used to baste the baked chicken breasts. This combination of seasonings brings out the sweetness of the chicken meat.

Menu 2 contrasts the taste of broccoli with the pungency of curry spices in the Indian-style salad. A tart *raita,* or yogurt condiment (here made with cucumber), and crisp toasted pita triangles are the accompaniments. You can prepare both the salad and the *raita* up to two days in advance without spoiling their texture or flavor.

In Menu 3, the vegetarian salad is composed of red and green pepper strips, tomato and egg wedges, and sprouts on a bed of brown rice. A mixture of fresh ginger, honey, and Japanese *miso* (soybean paste) is the dressing.

A woven tablecloth, dark wine glasses, and chopsticks add to the exotic mood of this one-dish meal. The chicken, vegetable, and noodle salad is carefully composed on a bed of leaf lettuce and garnished with fresh coriander.

Oriental Chicken, Vegetable, and Noodle Salad

For this Oriental salad, the cook uses a number of unusual ingredients, including *udon* or *soba* noodles (see page 10), macadamia nuts, Japanese eggplants, and fresh *shiitake* mushrooms. Originally imported from Japan, *shiitake* are now being grown in the United States under the name Golden Oak mushrooms. Fresh *shiitake* have wide dark-brown caps and small woody stems. They should be firm and feel dry. Layered in a container and covered with damp cheesecloth or paper towels, they can be refrigerated for a week. These mushrooms are sold at specialty food shops and many supermarkets.

Marble-sized macadamias, considered by many to be the world's finest nuts, are creamy white and slightly sweet. Because they are rich in oil, macadamias should be stored in the freezer.

Tiny Japanese eggplants, sold at quality greengrocers and some Oriental and Middle Eastern markets, are sweeter than Western varieties. They should be firm and have a rich, deep-purple color. Any type of baby eggplant could be substituted.

Despite its name, *tamari* is virtually unknown in Japan. Because *tamari* is brewed with very little wheat, it tends to have a fuller, stronger taste than other soy sauces. This dark, unrefined soy is available in most health food stores.

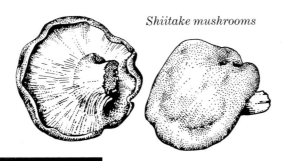

Shiitake mushrooms

WHAT TO DRINK

Tea, hot or iced, would accompany this dish perfectly. If you prefer wine with your meal, a good choice is a relatively full-bodied dry white California Chardonnay.

SHOPPING LIST AND STAPLES

2 skinless, boneless chicken breasts (about 1½ pounds total weight), halved
½ pound asparagus, or 2 small Japanese eggplants
¼ pound snow peas
Small head leaf lettuce
Small head Belgian endive
Small bunch fresh coriander
2 large fresh shiitake mushrooms
Large clove garlic
2-inch piece fresh ginger
1 cup plus 1 tablespoon Oriental sesame oil
⅔ cup rice vinegar
⅔ cup tamari or other soy sauce
2 tablespoons honey
7-ounce package Japanese udon or soba noodles
4½-ounce jar macadamia nuts or almonds
½ teaspoon ground coriander
Salt

UTENSILS

Stockpot or large kettle
Medium-size sauté pan with cover
12 x 9-inch baking sheet
Large bowl
Colander
Strainer
Measuring cups and spoons
Chef's knife
Paring knife
2 wooden spoons
Slotted spoon
Small whisk
Pastry brush
Grater

START-TO-FINISH STEPS

1. Follow salad recipe steps 1 through 16.
2. While chicken is cooling, follow salad recipe steps 17 through 19.
3. Follow salad recipe steps 20 and 21 and serve.

RECIPES

Oriental Chicken, Vegetable, and Noodle Salad

Dressing:
Large clove garlic
2-inch piece fresh ginger
1 cup Oriental sesame oil
⅔ cup rice vinegar

⅔ cup tamari or other soy sauce
½ teaspoon ground coriander
2 tablespoons honey

Salad:
2 skinless, boneless chicken breasts (about 1½ pounds total weight), halved
½ pound asparagus, or 2 small Japanese eggplants
2 tablespoons salt
Small bunch fresh coriander
1 cup snow peas
7-ounce package Japanese udon or soba noodles
Small head leaf lettuce
Small head Belgian endive
2 large fresh shiitake mushrooms
1 tablespoon Oriental sesame oil
½ cup macadamia nuts or almonds

1. Preheat oven to 350 degrees.
2. Peel and mince garlic. Peel and grate enough ginger to measure 2 heaping teaspoons.
3. In large bowl, combine sesame oil, vinegar, tamari, garlic, ginger, ground coriander, and honey. Whisk dressing until blended; set aside.
4. Lightly oil baking sheet.
5. Rinse chicken under cold running water and dry with paper towels. Place chicken breasts, smooth side up, on prepared baking sheet.
6. If using eggplants, rinse under cold running water and dry. Cut each eggplant lengthwise into quarters and place on baking sheet with chicken.
7. Liberally brush chicken and eggplant with dressing; reserve remaining dressing. Bake 30 minutes or until juices run clear when chicken is pierced with tip of knife.
8. While chicken and eggplant are baking, fill stockpot or kettle two-thirds full with cold water, add the salt, and bring to a boil over high heat.
9. Meanwhile, wash fresh coriander and dry with paper towels. Finely chop enough coriander to measure ⅔ cup and set aside for garnish. Reserve remainder for another use.
10. Wash snow peas, and asparagus if using, under cold running water. Trim off ends of snow peas and discard. Break off tough woody bottoms of asparagus; peel stalks, if desired.
11. Break noodles into thirds. Add to stockpot and boil 7 minutes.
12. While noodles are boiling, place snow peas in strainer and immerse in boiling noodle water for 30 seconds. Immediately refresh under cold running water, and turn onto paper towels to drain.
13. Repeat process for asparagus, but immerse 3 to 5 minutes, or until crisp-tender. Refresh under cold water and drain on paper towels.
14. Turn noodles into colander and drain. Transfer to large bowl with reserved dressing. Toss noodles gently until evenly coated and set aside.
15. Wash lettuce under cold running water and dry with paper towels. Remove and discard any bruised or dis-

colored leaves. Tear lettuce into bite-size pieces. Line 4 dinner plates with lettuce.
16. Remove chicken and eggplant from oven and set aside to cool slightly.
17. Meanwhile, rinse endive under cold water and dry with paper towel. Separate leaves; set aside.
18. Wash shiitake mushrooms under cold running water and dry with paper towels. Remove and discard tough end of stems. Cut mushrooms into thin slivers; set aside.
19. In medium-size sauté pan, heat 1 tablespoon sesame oil over low heat. Add mushrooms and nuts, and sauté, stirring and tossing, 5 minutes, or until mushrooms are lightly browned and soft. Remove pan from heat; set aside.
20. When chicken is cool enough to handle, cut crosswise into ¼-inch-wide strips.
21. With slotted spoon, arrange equal portions of marinated noodles in center of each lettuce-lined plate. Top one half of noodles with chicken slices and the other half with mushrooms and nuts. Arrange endive, snow peas, and asparagus spears or eggplant quarters around noodles, and pour remaining marinade over salad. Garnish with chopped coriander and serve immediately.

ADDED TOUCH

These toasted slices of French bread with roasted vegetables supplement a salad meal. Let your guests assemble open-faced sandwiches: First, squeeze the cooked garlic out of its skin and spread it on the bread; then spread a layer of roasted eggplant over the garlic, and top with a piece of red pepper.

French Bread with Roasted Garlic and Vegetables

6 tablespoons olive oil, approximately
2 Japanese eggplants
2 large red bell peppers
2 heads garlic
1 loaf French bread

1. Preheat oven to 350 degrees. Lightly oil a 12 x 9-inch baking sheet.
2. Wash eggplants under cold running water and dry with paper towels. Quarter each eggplant lengthwise and place on prepared baking sheet.
3. Wash bell peppers and dry with paper towels. Halve, core, and seed peppers. Cut each half into quarters and place on baking sheet.
4. Trim off top fourth from garlic heads to expose the cloves. Place on baking sheet.
5. Brush vegetables liberally with olive oil and roast 30 minutes, or until peppers are limp and eggplant and garlic are slightly brown.
6. During the last 5 minutes of roasting, place loaf of French bread, unwrapped, in oven and heat.
7. Cut warm bread on diagonal into 2-inch-thick slices. With spatula, divide vegetables equally among 4 plates and serve accompanied by bread.

Curried Broccoli Salad with Pita Toasts
Cucumber Raita

A chilled salad of curried broccoli with toasted pita bread triangles and cucumber raita are ideal hot-weather fare.

An Indian meal is considered incomplete without a dish made with yogurt, such as *raita*. A *raita* can be made with yogurt and any type of raw or cooked vegetables or fruit. This one, called *kheere ka raita,* uses a seedless English hothouse cucumber, which is a relative newcomer to American produce stands. Choose a cucumber that is firm and green, without any soft or shriveled spots. Refrigerate it in the plastic wrap in which it is sold, and use it within a week. Hothouse cucumbers are longer than standard varieties, and because their smooth skin is unwaxed, they do not require peeling.

The cooking liquid for the broccoli calls for apple juice, which adds sweetness to the curry and eliminates any bitter aftertaste from the spices. You can substitute cauliflower for the broccoli if you prefer; it will take on the yellow curry color.

WHAT TO DRINK

The cook suggests a cold, light beer or iced tea as the best beverage with this Indian-style meal.

SHOPPING LIST AND STAPLES

8-ounce package frozen tiny shrimp
2 heads broccoli
4 large mushrooms (about ¼ pound total weight)
Large onion
Medium-size carrot
1 hothouse cucumber (about ¾ pound)
1 head Boston lettuce
1 large clove garlic
1-inch piece fresh ginger
2 tablespoons unsalted butter
1 pint plain yogurt
½ pint sour cream
1 pint apple juice
1 tablespoon Oriental sesame oil
3 tablespoons honey
4 round pita breads
6-ounce package dried grated unsweetened coconut
4-ounce jar raw peanuts
3 teaspoons ground turmeric
1 teaspoon ground cardamom
2 teaspoons cumin seeds
1½ teaspoons yellow mustard seeds
½ teaspoon cinnamon
1 teaspoon ground coriander
1 teaspoon Cayenne pepper, approximately
½ teaspoon ground cumin
½ teaspoon caraway seeds
Salt

UTENSILS

Food processor (optional)
Large heavy-gauge skillet with cover
Small nonstick heavy-gauge skillet
Medium-size saucepan with cover
Baking sheet
Large bowl
Medium-size bowl
Salad spinner (optional)
Colander or large strainer
Measuring cups and spoons
Chef's knife
Paring knife
2 wooden spoons
Kitchen scissors
Grater

START-TO-FINISH STEPS

One hour ahead: Immerse frozen shrimp for salad recipe in bowl of cold water to thaw.

1. Follow salad recipe steps 1 through 14.
2. Follow raita recipe steps 1 through 5.
3. Follow salad recipe steps 15 through 17, and serve with chilled raita.

RECIPES

Curried Broccoli Salad with Pita Toasts

2 heads broccoli
¾ cup apple juice
Large onion
1 large clove garlic
Medium-size carrot
1-inch piece fresh ginger
4 large mushrooms (about ¼ pound total weight)
2 tablespoons unsalted butter
1 tablespoon Oriental sesame oil
½ teaspoon caraway seeds
3 teaspoons ground turmeric
1 teaspoon ground coriander
1 teaspoon ground cardamom
½ teaspoon ground cumin
½ teaspoon cinnamon
1½ teaspoons yellow mustard seeds
1 teaspoon salt
1 teaspoon Cayenne pepper, approximately
8-ounce package frozen tiny shrimp, thawed
3 tablespoons honey
½ cup raw peanuts
4 round pita breads
1 head Boston lettuce
2 to 4 tablespoons dried grated unsweetened coconut

1. Rinse broccoli under cold running water. Trim off stems and reserve for another use. Cut broccoli into florets. You should have about 6 cups.
2. In medium-size saucepan, combine broccoli, apple juice, and ½ cup water, and bring to a boil over high heat.
3. Meanwhile, halve and peel onion. Cut one half crosswise into ⅛-inch-thick slices. You will have about ¾ cup. Reserve remaining half for another use. Peel and mince

enough garlic to measure 1 tablespoon; set aside.

4. Cover broccoli, reduce heat to medium-low, and simmer gently about 5 minutes, or until crisp-tender.

5. While broccoli is cooking, peel and trim carrot. Halve crosswise, then cut each half lengthwise. Cut quarters into ¼-inch julienne; set aside.

6. Using coarse side of grater, grate enough unpeeled ginger to measure 1 tablespoon.

7. Turn broccoli into colander or large strainer set over large bowl and immediately refresh under cold running water; reserve cooking liquid.

8. Wipe mushrooms with damp paper towels. Cut into ¼-inch-thick slices; set aside. You should have about 1 cup.

9. Preheat oven to 250 degrees.

10. In large heavy-gauge skillet, melt butter over medium heat. Stir in sesame oil, caraway seeds, turmeric, coriander, cardamom, cumin, cinnamon, mustard seeds, salt, and Cayenne to taste. Cover skillet and heat until seeds begin to pop.

11. Stir in onion, ginger, and mushrooms, and sauté over medium-high heat about 1 minute, or until onion begins to soften but not brown.

12. Stir in garlic and carrot, and sauté another minute.

13. Add broccoli and cooking liquid and bring to a boil over high heat. Boil, uncovered, 2 minutes, or until liquid is reduced to 1 cup. Rinse and dry bowl.

14. Remove skillet from heat. Stir in shrimp, honey, and peanuts. Turn salad into large dry bowl, cover, and chill.

15. With kitchen scissors, cut each pita into quarters and arrange on baking sheet. Toast 10 minutes, or until crisp.

16. While pitas are toasting, wash lettuce and dry in salad spinner or with paper towels. Remove and discard any bruised or discolored leaves. Divide among 4 dinner plates.

17. Remove salad from refrigerator. Divide among lettuce-lined plates and sprinkle with grated coconut to taste. Serve with toasted pita.

Cucumber Raita

1 hothouse cucumber (about ¾ pound)
2 cups plain yogurt
1 cup sour cream
2 teaspoons cumin seeds
2 teaspoons salt

1. Wash and dry cucumber. Halve unpeeled cucumber crosswise; reserve one half for another use.

2. Using coarse side of grater, grate half of cucumber and place in medium-size bowl.

3. Add yogurt and sour cream to cucumber and stir to combine.

4. In small nonstick heavy-gauge skillet, toast cumin seeds over medium heat, shaking pan to avoid scorching, about 2 minutes, or until they release their fragrance. Stir in salt.

5. Add salted cumin seeds to yogurt mixture and stir to combine. Cover with plastic wrap and refrigerate raita until ready to serve.

■■■■■
ADDED TOUCH

For a traditional accompaniment to the curried salad, serve currant and grape chutney. If the grapes are very sweet, you may want to use less honey; sample the chutney as it cooks and add honey to taste.

Sweet Currant and Green Grape Chutney

Medium-size clove garlic
2-inch piece fresh ginger
1¼ pounds seedless green grapes
¾ cup apple juice
1 teaspoon cinnamon
1 teaspoon ground cardamom
1 cup currants
⅔ cup honey
⅔ cup apple cider vinegar

1. Peel and mince enough garlic to measure 1 teaspoon. Using grater, grate enough unpeeled ginger to measure 2 tablespoons.

2. Rinse grapes under cold running water and drain; dry with paper towels. Remove enough grapes from stems to measure 3 cups.

3. Combine all ingredients in a small heavy-gauge saucepan and bring to a boil over high heat. Continue to boil mixture, uncovered, 5 minutes.

4. Remove pan from heat and set aside to cool slightly.

5. Purée mixture in two batches in food processor, or in blender.

6. Return chutney to saucepan and bring to a boil over high heat. Reduce heat and simmer 10 minutes.

7. Pour chutney into strainer set over medium-size bowl; do *not* press. Discard any liquid drained from chutney.

8. Turn chutney into small bowl and serve warm, or cover and chill in refrigerator before serving.

Vegetarian Chef's Salad with Creamy Miso-Ginger Dressing
Savory Herb and Cheese Muffins

For a wholesome lunch or light dinner, serve this colorful meal-in-a-bowl with savory cheese-enriched muffins.

This robust salad contains brown rice, an unmilled grain with its nutritive outer bran layer intact. Brown rice takes longer to cook than white rice, but it still retains a pleasant nutty taste. To avoid using two pots, boil the rice and eggs together: The rice sinks to the bottom of the pot, and when the eggs finish cooking, you can easily lift them out of the pot without disturbing the rice.

WHAT TO DRINK

A light semi-dry white wine would suit this menu well. A California French Colombard or a slightly sweet California Chenin Blanc would also be good.

SHOPPING LIST AND STAPLES

2 medium-size tomatoes (about 1 pound total weight)
1 red bell pepper
1 green bell pepper
1 bunch scallions
2 ounces mixed sprouts, such as alfalfa, mung bean, or soybean
4 large cloves garlic

1-inch piece fresh ginger
Small bunch fresh parsley
Small bunch each fresh basil, dill, marjoram, and thyme, or 1 tablespoon each dried
1 lemon
6 extra-large eggs
½ pint buttermilk
2 tablespoons unsalted butter
¾ pound Monterey Jack or Swiss cheese
2 ounces Parmesan cheese
¼ cup olive oil
¾ cup sesame or safflower oil
¼ cup safflower oil, or 1 cup if not using sesame oil
¼ cup apple cider vinegar, or ½ cup if not using raspberry vinegar
¼ cup raspberry vinegar (optional)
3 tablespoons tamari or other soy sauce
1½ tablespoons white miso paste
¼ cup honey
1 pound long- or short-grain brown rice
2 cups all-purpose flour, plus flour for dusting pan
3 teaspoons baking powder

¾ teaspoon dry mustard
¼ teaspoon ground coriander
Salt
Freshly ground white pepper

UTENSILS

Food processor or blender
Large heavy-gauge saucepan with cover
Small heavy-gauge saucepan
12-cup muffin pan
2 large bowls
Medium-size bowl
Colander
Strainer
Measuring cups and spoons
Chef's knife
Paring knife
2 wooden spoons
Slotted spoon
Rubber spatula
2 whisks
Cooling rack
Flour sifter
Grater

START-TO-FINISH STEPS

About one-half hour ahead: Set out eggs for muffin recipe to come to room temperature.

1. Wash parsley for salad recipe, and fresh herbs if using for muffin recipe, and dry with paper towels. Mince enough parsley to measure ¼ cup. Mince enough basil, marjoram, thyme, and dill to measure 2 tablespoons each.
2. Follow salad recipe steps 1 and 2.
3. While eggs are cooking, follow muffin recipe steps 1 through 5.
4. Follow salad recipe steps 3 and 4.
5. While rice is cooking, follow muffin recipe steps 6 through 8.
6. While muffins are baking, follow salad recipe steps 5 through 13.
7. Follow muffin recipe step 9 and salad recipe step 14.
8. When muffins have cooled slightly, follow salad recipe step 15 and serve with muffins.

RECIPES

Vegetarian Chef's Salad with Creamy Miso-Ginger Dressing

2 cups long- or short-grain brown rice
2 extra-large eggs
1 bunch scallions
4 large cloves garlic
1 lemon
¼ cup minced parsley
¾ teaspoon dry mustard

¼ cup apple cider vinegar
½ teaspoon salt
¼ teaspoon freshly ground white pepper
¼ cup olive oil
¼ cup safflower oil
1 red bell pepper
1 green bell pepper
2 medium-size tomatoes (about 1 pound total weight)
1 cup mixed sprouts, such as alfalfa, mung bean, or soybean
2 ounces Parmesan cheese

Dressing:
1-inch piece fresh ginger
1½ tablespoons white miso paste
¾ cup sesame or safflower oil
¼ cup raspberry or apple cider vinegar
3 tablespoons tamari or other soy sauce
¼ teaspoon ground coriander
2 tablespoons honey

1. In large heavy-gauge saucepan, combine rice and 4 cups cold water and bring to a boil over medium-high heat.
2. Add eggs to boiling water; reduce heat to medium and cook, uncovered, 10 minutes.
3. Using slotted spoon, transfer eggs to colander and rinse under cold running water; set aside to cool.
4. Continue cooking rice, uncovered, another 10 minutes.
5. Check level of rice cooking liquid; it should be just even with level of rice. If not, add water. Cover pan, reduce heat to very low, and simmer very gently 25 more minutes until rice has absorbed liquid.
6. Meanwhile, wash and dry scallions. Mince scallions to measure about ½ cup; set aside. Peel and mince garlic. Squeeze enough lemon juice to measure 2 tablespoons.
7. Combine scallions, garlic, parsley, dry mustard, ¼ cup cider vinegar, lemon juice, salt, white pepper, olive oil, and safflower oil in large bowl, and whisk until blended; set aside.
8. Wash and dry bell peppers. Halve, core, and seed peppers. Reserve one half of each pepper for another use. Cut remaining halves lengthwise into ¼-inch-wide strips.
9. Wash tomatoes and dry with paper towels. Core and halve tomatoes. Cut each half into quarters; set aside. Place sprouts in strainer, rinse, and set aside to drain.
10. In food processor fitted with steel blade or with grater, grate enough Parmesan to measure ½ cup; set aside. Rinse and dry processor bowl.
11. Using coarse side of grater, grate enough unpeeled ginger to measure 1 teaspoon for dressing.
12. In food processor or blender, combine miso, oil, vinegar, tamari, 3 tablespoons cold water, ginger, coriander, and honey, and process until thick and creamy; set aside.
13. Peel eggs and cut lengthwise into quarters; set aside.
14. When rice is cooked, turn into bowl with scallion mixture. Add Parmesan and toss to combine.
15. Turn warm rice into large salad bowl. Top with tomatoes, sprouts, pepper strips, and egg quarters. Pour creamy dressing over salad and serve.

Savory Herb and Cheese Muffins

¾ pound Monterey Jack or Swiss cheese
2 tablespoons unsalted butter
2 cups all-purpose flour, plus flour for dusting pan
3 teaspoons baking powder
½ teaspoon salt
4 extra-large eggs, at room temperature
1 cup buttermilk
2 tablespoons honey
2 tablespoons each minced fresh basil, dill, marjoram, and thyme, or 1 tablespoon each dried

1. Preheat oven to 400 degrees.
2. Using food processor fitted with shredding disk, or grater, shred enough cheese to measure 3 cups; set aside.
3. In small heavy-gauge saucepan, melt butter over low heat.
4. Lightly oil a 12-cup muffin pan and dust with flour.
5. Sift 2 cups flour, baking powder, and salt into large bowl; set aside.
6. In medium-size bowl, combine eggs and buttermilk, and whisk until frothy. Add melted butter and honey, and whisk briefly to combine.
7. Fold wet ingredients into dry ingredients. Add herbs and cheese, and stir just until blended; do *not* overmix.
8. Spoon batter into prepared muffin pan, filling each cup two-thirds full, and bake 20 to 25 minutes, or until muffins are lightly browned and springy to the touch.
9. Turn muffins out onto rack and let cool before serving.

ADDED TOUCHES

These piquant, bite-sized hors d'oeuvres are easy to prepare. The marinated hearts keep for up to two weeks in the refrigerator.

Baked Artichoke Hearts

4 medium-size artichokes
3 tablespoons cream cheese
3 tablespoons freshly grated Parmesan cheese
⅔ cup safflower or olive oil
⅓ cup raspberry vinegar or red wine vinegar
1 tablespoon minced fresh oregano, or 1 teaspoon dried
2 tablespoons minced fresh basil, or 2 teaspoons dried

1. In large stockpot, bring 6 quarts water to a boil.
2. While water is coming to a boil, rinse artichokes under cold running water. Quarter artichokes lengthwise.
3. Place cream cheese in small bowl and set aside to soften. Place Parmesan on flat plate; set aside.
4. Add artichokes to boiling water and boil 10 minutes.
5. Using tongs, transfer artichokes to colander and set aside to cool slightly.
6. Meanwhile, combine oil, vinegar, and herbs in medium-size bowl; set aside.
7. When artichokes are cool enough to handle, trim stems, cut back leaves halfway, and remove hairy choke; discard stems and leaves. Add artichoke hearts to oil and vinegar, and marinate 30 minutes.

8. Preheat oven to 350 degrees.
9. Lightly oil baking sheet.
10. Remove artichokes from marinade and drain. Spread cut sides of each quarter with ½ teaspoon cream cheese, roll in Parmesan, and place on prepared baking sheet.
11. Bake artichokes 10 to 12 minutes. Serve hot.

This frothy mousse of puréed fresh berries contains tangy fresh lemon juice and sweet maple syrup. For an even more refreshing dessert, chill the glasses.

Lemon-Berry Mousse

3 medium-size lemons
1 pint strawberries or raspberries
2 large eggs
3 tablespoons arrowroot or cornstarch
⅔ cup maple syrup
1 cup heavy cream
½ teaspoon vanilla extract
¼ teaspoon ground cardamom
1 whole nutmeg

1. Place bowl for whipping cream in freezer to chill.
2. Rinse and dry 2 lemons. Using zester or grater, remove enough rind to measure 2 tablespoons.
3. Squeeze enough lemon juice to measure ½ cup.
4. Rinse berries under cold running water and dry. If using strawberries, remove stems and discard.
5. In food processor or blender, purée 1 cup of berries; set aside.
6. Separate eggs, placing yolks in small heavy-gauge saucepan and whites in large bowl; set aside whites.
7. Add arrowroot or cornstarch, lemon juice, lemon rind, and maple syrup to yolks, and whisk until blended. Whisk in puréed berries.
8. Whisking vigorously, heat berry mixture over low heat, 5 to 6 minutes, or until mixture has reached the consistency of pudding.
9. Turn mixture into stainless-steel bowl, cover, and place in freezer to chill 10 minutes.
10. Rinse and dry mint sprigs, if using; set aside.
11. Beat egg whites with electric mixer until stiff. Rinse beaters in cold water; chill in freezer about 5 minutes.
12. Place heavy cream in chilled bowl and beat with electric mixer at high speed until stiff. Gently stir in vanilla and cardamom.
13. Using rubber spatula, fold whites into whipped cream.
14. Remove berry mixture from freezer and gently fold into whipped cream mixture. Cover and return bowl to freezer for at least 1 hour before serving.
15. If using strawberries, thinly slice all but 4 of the remaining berries and line bottoms of 4 parfait glasses or large goblets with sliced berries. If using raspberries, reserve 4 berries for garnish and place an equal portion of whole berries in bottom of each dessert glass. Divide mousse among glasses and top each serving with 1 whole berry and a grating of nutmeg.

Victoria Wise

V ictoria Wise spent her childhood in Japan and later lived in the south of France, where she apprenticed in a charcuterie—the French version of a butcher shop. This diverse background has influenced her cooking and menu planning: She uses classic French cooking techniques, yet handles her ingredients with a characteristic Oriental lightness.

Today, Victoria Wise lives in California, where she often creates salads with vegetables from her own garden. The ham, spinach, and potato salad of Menu 2 is perfect for an early-fall luncheon, when spinach is just up and new red potatoes are ready to be dug. She mixes the spinach with slices of smoked ham, but you can also make the salad with any mild smoked meat, such as pork loin, chicken, or turkey. When new red potatoes are out of season, use waxy white potatoes or colorful sweet potatoes.

In Menu 1 she offers fresh tuna Niçoise—a salad reminiscent of her days in Provence. Niçoise dishes are usually garnished with anchovies and black olives, and this salad is no exception. It is best when the basic ingredients—tomatoes, green beans, and sweet basil—are in season.

The cook describes the shrimp and *fusilli* (corkscrew pasta) salad of Menu 3 as "in keeping with Americans' recent craving for pasta in any form." She dresses the salad with a pesto sauce made with fresh spinach as well as basil. Garlic bread is the accompaniment.

An oval earthenware platter makes an ideal serving dish for this carefully assembled Niçoise salad: Greens form a leafy bed for the tomatoes, green beans, bell pepper strips, potatoes, and chunks of tuna steak garnished with anchovies, capers, and Niçoise olives. French bread, lightly toasted with feta cheese on top, is served in a rustic basket.

Fresh Tuna Niçoise
French Bread with Feta Cheese and Olive Oil

Although canned white albacore and light yellowfin tuna are popular salad ingredients, few cooks think of using succulent fresh tuna steaks. Sold at many fish markets, fresh tuna looks like raw beef. It should not smell sour and should have moist elastic flesh. Refrigerate tuna steaks loosely wrapped in plastic, and use them as soon as possible. When they cook, they become firm and develop a strong but not unpleasant flavor. For the best results, allow the tuna to cool for at least 20 minutes after cooking, and serve it at room temperature in the salad. If fresh tuna is unavailable, use canned water-packed white-meat albacore.

A mainstay of Greek cuisine, feta cheese is soft and crumbly, with a characteristic sharp, astringent taste. It is sold at delicatessen counters in most supermarkets and will stay fresh in the refrigerator for months if stored in salty water. Rinse it under cold water before using.

WHAT TO DRINK

A full-bodied white wine or a dry rosé, well chilled, is the best choice for this Provençal meal. Try a California Chardonnay or French Mâcon. For the rosé, purchase one from the south of France if possible. Tavel is excellent.

SHOPPING LIST AND STAPLES

Three ¾- to 1-inch-thick fresh tuna steaks
   (about 1½ pounds total weight)
¾ pound small red or white potatoes
¾ pound ripe tomatoes
½ pound green beans
1 head Boston lettuce, 1 bunch watercress, 1 pound
   spinach, or combination of these greens
Small green bell pepper
Small bunch scallions
3 medium-size cloves garlic
Small bunch fresh basil
1 lemon
¼ pound feta cheese
1½ cups plus 1 tablespoon olive oil
⅓ cup red wine vinegar
7-ounce jar Niçoise or oil-cured black olives
2-ounce jar capers
2-ounce tin anchovy fillets, preferably salt-packed
1 baguette, or eight 1-inch-thick slices regular
   French bread

1 bay leaf
Salt and freshly ground black pepper

UTENSILS

2 medium-size saucepans, one with cover
13 x 9-inch baking sheet
13 x 9-inch nonaluminum baking dish
Large bowl
2 medium-size bowls
2 small bowls
Salad spinner (optional)
Colander
Strainer
Measuring cups and spoons
Chef's knife
Bread knife
Paring knife
2 wooden spoons
Whisk

START-TO-FINISH STEPS

1. Follow tuna Niçoise recipe steps 1 through 24.
2. Follow French bread recipe steps 1 through 5 and serve with salad.

RECIPES

Fresh Tuna Niçoise

Three ¾- to 1-inch-thick fresh tuna steaks (about 1½
   pounds total weight)
1 lemon
Salt and freshly ground black pepper
1 cup plus 1 tablespoon olive oil
¾ pound small red or white potatoes
3 medium-size cloves garlic
½ cup Niçoise or oil-cured black olives
1 bay leaf
½ pound green beans
1 head Boston lettuce, 1 bunch watercress, 1 pound
   spinach, or combination of these greens
2-ounce jar capers
⅓ cup red wine vinegar
Small bunch fresh basil
¾ pound ripe tomatoes
Small green bell pepper

Small bunch scallions
2-ounce tin anchovy fillets, preferably salt-packed

1. Preheat oven to 375 degrees.
2. Place tuna steaks in nonaluminum baking dish in a single layer. Halve lemon crosswise and squeeze juice of one half over steaks; reserve remaining half for another use. Sprinkle steaks lightly with salt and pepper and drizzle with 3 tablespoons olive oil. Turn steaks to coat both sides and set aside to marinate at least 15 minutes.
3. Wash potatoes under cold running water. Cut unpeeled potatoes crosswise into ½-inch-thick rounds and place in medium-size saucepan. Add enough cold water to cover potatoes by 3 inches and bring to a boil over high heat.
4. Fill another medium-size saucepan two-thirds full with cold water, cover, and bring to a boil over high heat.
5. Crush 1 clove garlic under blade of chef's knife; remove and discard peel. In small bowl, combine olives, crushed garlic, bay leaf, and 2 tablespoons olive oil; toss to combine. Set aside to marinate.
6. Wash green beans under cold running water. Trim ends and discard. Cut beans lengthwise into halves or thirds, depending on size.
7. Reduce heat under potatoes to medium and cook 10 to 15 minutes, or until they can be pierced easily with tip of knife.
8. Add green beans to boiling water and cook 3 to 5 minutes, or until crisp-tender.
9. While beans are cooking, place tuna steaks on middle rack of oven and bake 8 minutes, or until opaque on outside and still pink in center.
10. Turn beans into strainer and refresh under cold running water; set aside to cool.
11. Wash greens and dry in salad spinner or with paper towels. Tear into bite-size pieces, wrap in paper towels, and refrigerate until ready to assemble salad.
12. Remove tuna from oven and set aside to cool. Raise oven temperature to 450 degrees.
13. Turn potatoes into colander and refresh under cold running water; set aside to cool.
14. For dressing, crush remaining 2 cloves garlic under blade of chef's knife; discard peel. Drain 1 tablespoon capers and rinse under cold running water; chop coarsely. Combine garlic, capers, and red wine vinegar in small bowl. Whisking continuously, add remaining ¾ cup olive oil in a slow, steady stream and whisk until blended. Add ¼ teaspoon salt, and freshly ground black pepper to taste, and whisk until blended; set aside.

15. Wash and dry basil. Cut leaves crosswise into ¼-inch-wide shreds to measure about ¾ cup; set aside.
16. Wash tomatoes and dry with paper towels. Core and quarter tomatoes. Halve each quarter crosswise.
17. Wash and dry green pepper. Core, halve, and seed pepper. Cut each half crosswise, then slice each quarter into ¼-inch-wide strips; set aside.
18. Wash and dry scallions. Thinly slice scallions to measure about 1 cup; set aside.
19. Combine potatoes, green pepper, scallions, and half of basil in large bowl. Add a few tablespoons of dressing and toss to combine.
20. Combine tomatoes and remaining basil in medium-size bowl. Add a tablespoon of dressing and toss to combine.
21. Dry green beans with paper towels and place in another medium-size bowl. Add a tablespoon of dressing and toss to combine.
22. If using salt-packed anchovies, rinse thoroughly under cold running water, gently rubbing off salt with your fingers. Halve lengthwise and pull out bone. Rinse again and pat dry. If using oil-packed anchovies, rinse gently and pat dry with paper towels. Set anchovies aside.
23. Remove skin from tuna steaks and discard; break tuna into large chunks.
24. Line platter with salad greens. Spoon tuna into center of platter and arrange potatoes, tomatoes, and green beans in mounds around tuna. Top tuna with anchovy fillets and dot platter with olives. Pour remaining dressing over salad and set aside until ready to serve.

French Bread with Feta Cheese and Olive Oil

1 baguette, or eight 1-inch-thick slices regular
  French bread
¼ pound feta cheese
½ cup olive oil

1. Halve baguette crosswise and then lengthwise.
2. Arrange bread on baking sheet in a single layer.
3. Place half of feta cheese in small bowl, reserving remainder for another use. Crumble feta with fork; you will have about 1 cup. Add olive oil, and, using fork or whisk, blend with feta.
4. Spoon mixture over cut surfaces of baguette, or on one side of French bread slices, and toast in 450-degree oven about 4 minutes, or just until feta is golden.
5. Transfer hot bread to napkin-lined basket or bowl.

Smoked Ham and Fresh Spinach Salad
with Creamy Mustard Mayonnaise
Deep-Fried Onion Rings

Crisp fried onion rings complement ham, spinach, and potato salad with creamy mustard mayonnaise dressing.

When deep fried, the onion rings remain moist and tender under their crisp batter coating. For successful deep frying, slice the onions uniformly so that they cook at the same rate. Beat the eggs thoroughly, and be sure to coat the onions completely with egg and then the flour. If you do not have a deep-fat thermometer, you can test the oil by combining a spoonful of egg and flour to make a small ball of batter, then dropping it into the hot fat. If the batter sizzles on contact, the fat has reached the right frying temperature. Do not fry too many onion rings at one time; they should fit on the surface of the oil without crowding. Batter coat other vegetables, such as eggplant slices, broccoli, cauliflower florets, or zucchini cut lengthwise, to create an Italian-style deep-fry platter.

WHAT TO DRINK

These dishes would go well with a light, fruity red wine. The cook suggests Beaujolais. Other options are a young California Zinfandel, a Gamay Beaujolais, or an Italian Chianti or Dolcetto.

SHOPPING LIST AND STAPLES

¾ pound mild smoked ham, such as Westphalian, sliced ⅛ inch thick
¾ pound small red potatoes
2 large yellow onions (about 1½ pounds total weight)
2 large bunches spinach (1½ to 2 pounds total weight)

Small bunch fresh chives or scallions
Small bunch fresh parsley
Small bunch fresh tarragon, or ¼ teaspoon dried
4 eggs
½ pint heavy cream
6 cups peanut oil
¾ cup mayonnaise, preferably homemade (see page 12)
4 teaspoons Dijon mustard
2 cups all-purpose flour
Salt
Freshly ground black pepper

UTENSILS

Large, deep heavy-gauge skillet
Medium-size saucepan
Shallow baking dish or brown bag
Large heatproof platter
Large bowl
Small bowl
Salad spinner (optional)
Colander
Mesh strainer
Measuring cups and spoons
Chef's knife
Paring knife
Whisk (optional)
Metal tongs (optional)
Deep-fat thermometer

START-TO-FINISH STEPS

1. Follow ham and spinach recipe step 1 and onion rings recipe step 1.
2. Follow ham and spinach recipe steps 2 through 8.
3. Follow onion rings recipe steps 2 through 8.
4. Follow ham and spinach recipe step 9, onion rings recipe step 9, and serve.

RECIPES

Smoked Ham and Fresh Spinach Salad with Creamy Mustard Mayonnaise

¾ pound small red potatoes
2 large bunches spinach (1½ to 2 pounds total weight)
Small bunch fresh parsley
Small bunch fresh tarragon, or ¼ teaspoon dried
Small bunch fresh chives or scallions
¾ cup mayonnaise
4 teaspoons Dijon mustard
2 tablespoons heavy cream
¾ pound mild smoked ham, such as Westphalian, sliced
    ⅛ inch thick
Freshly ground black pepper

1. Wash potatoes and slice into ¼-inch-thick rounds. Place in medium-size saucepan with enough cold water to cover potatoes by 3 inches and bring to a boil over high heat.

2. When water comes to a boil, reduce heat to medium and cook, uncovered, 10 to 15 minutes, or until potatoes can be pierced easily with tip of sharp knife.
3. While potatoes are boiling, remove and discard stems from smaller spinach leaves, reserving large leaves for another use. Wash spinach thoroughly in several changes of cold water and dry in salad spinner or with paper towels. Line 4 plates with spinach leaves and set aside.
4. Transfer potatoes to colander and set aside to cool.
5. Wash parsley, and fresh tarragon if using, and dry with paper towels. Trim and discard stems from parsley and chop enough to measure 2 tablespoons; set aside. Reserve 4 sprigs tarragon for garnish, and coarsely chop enough remaining tarragon to measure 1 teaspoon; set aside. Reserve remaining herbs for another use.
6. Wash chives or scallions and dry with paper towels. Chop enough chives to measure 1 tablespoon. If using scallions, trim ends and discard. Chop enough green tops to measure 1 tablespoon; reserve remaining scallions for another use.
7. In small bowl, combine mayonnaise, mustard, cream, tarragon, and chives or scallions, and stir with fork until blended; set aside.
8. To assemble salad, loosely roll each slice of ham into cone shape and arrange slices in center of each spinach-lined plate. Arrange potatoes on either side of ham and sprinkle with freshly ground black pepper to taste.
9. Drizzle each salad with 2 tablespoons creamy mustard mayonnaise, sprinkle with parsley, and serve remaining dressing on the side.

Deep-Fried Onion Rings

2 large yellow onions (about 1½ pounds total weight)
4 eggs
6 cups peanut oil
2 cups all-purpose flour
Salt

1. Peel and cut onions crosswise into ¼-inch-thick rounds. Separate into rings, discarding green centers; set aside.
2. Preheat oven to 200 degrees.
3. Break eggs into large bowl. Add ¼ cup water and beat with fork or whisk until blended.
4. Add onion rings to egg mixture and stir with fork until well coated.
5. Pour peanut oil into large, deep heavy-gauge skillet and place skillet over medium-high heat.
6. Place flour in shallow baking dish or brown bag.
7. Line a heatproof platter with paper towels.
8. When oil registers 375 degrees on deep-fat thermometer, dredge onion rings, a handful at a time, in flour. Using tongs or mesh strainer, carefully lower rings into hot oil and deep fry, adjusting heat as necessary to keep temperature constant, about 3 minutes, or until golden. With mesh strainer, transfer onion rings to paper-towel-lined platter and keep warm in oven until ready to serve.
9. Just before serving, sprinkle onion rings lightly with salt and divide among 4 salad plates.

Shrimp and Pasta with Spinach Pesto
Italian Bread with Garlic, Thyme, and Olive Oil

Cooked shrimp form a decorative pinwheel on top of the salad of corkscrew pasta and fresh peas tossed with spinach pesto. Crusty bread coated with garlic, thyme, and olive oil is a fitting partner for the salad.

Pesto, which originated in the city of Genoa, is a zesty uncooked herb sauce traditionally containing fresh basil, garlic, olive oil, Parmesan or Romano cheese, and pine nuts. It can be used as a pasta topping, a sauce for grilled meats or freshly sliced tomatoes, or as a garnish for soups and salads. The cook provides an unexpected twist to the standard pesto recipe by adding spinach, which intensifies the flavor of the fresh basil. When basil is out of season, substitute an equal amount of fresh parsley plus 1 teaspoon dried oregano or tarragon.

WHAT TO DRINK

The cook recommends a light Chianti with this menu, but you could also try a crisp acidic white wine such as Verdicchio or Pinot Grigio.

SHOPPING LIST AND STAPLES

1 to 1½ pounds medium-size shrimp (about 28 shrimp)
1½ pounds fresh peas, or 10-ounce package frozen
1 bunch fresh spinach (about 1 pound)
Medium-size yellow onion
8 cloves garlic
Small bunch fresh basil
Small bunch fresh thyme, or 2½ teaspoons dried
¼ pound Parmesan cheese
1½ cups olive oil
1 cup tarragon vinegar
¾ pound dry fusilli, shells, or linguine
1 long loaf Italian bread
2 bay leaves
Salt and freshly ground black pepper
6 peppercorns
2 cups dry white wine

UTENSILS

Food processor or blender
Stockpot
Medium-size skillet
Large nonaluminum saucepan with cover
Baking sheet
Large bowl
3 small bowls
Colander
Large sieve

Large mesh strainer
Measuring cups and spoons
Chef's knife
Bread knife
Paring knife
2 wooden spoons
Garlic press
Pastry brush
Grater (if not using processor)

START-TO-FINISH STEPS

1. For shrimp and pasta recipe, peel 4 cloves garlic and put through garlic press held over small bowl. Repeat for remaining 4 cloves garlic and place in another small bowl for bread recipe. If using fresh thyme, rinse and dry with paper towels. Reserve 6 sprigs for shrimp and pasta recipe and strip enough leaves from remainder to measure 2 tablespoons for bread recipe.
2. Follow shrimp and pasta recipe steps 1 through 13 and bread recipe step 1.
3. Follow shrimp and pasta recipe steps 14 through 18.
4. Follow bread recipe steps 2 through 4.
5. While bread is toasting, follow shrimp and pasta recipe step 19.
6. Follow bread recipe step 5 and serve with shrimp and pasta.

RECIPES

Shrimp and Pasta with Spinach Pesto

Medium-size yellow onion
6 peppercorns
6 sprigs fresh thyme, or ½ teaspoon dried
2 bay leaves
1 cup tarragon vinegar
2 cups dry white wine
1½ pounds fresh peas, or 10-ounce package frozen
1 to 1½ pounds medium-size shrimp (about 28 shrimp)
¾ pound dry fusilli, shells, or linguine
1 bunch fresh spinach (about 1 pound)
Small bunch fresh basil
¼ pound Parmesan cheese
4 cloves garlic, peeled and pressed
1 cup olive oil
Salt
Freshly ground black pepper

1. Peel and halve onion. Coarsely chop one half; reserve remaining half for another use.
2. Crack peppercorns under flat blade of chef's knife.
3. Combine onion, cracked peppercorns, thyme, bay leaves, vinegar, white wine, and 8 cups cold water in large nonaluminum saucepan and bring to a boil, partially covered, over high heat.
4. Meanwhile, fill stockpot two-thirds full with cold water and bring to a boil over high heat.
5. Shell fresh peas, if using.

6. Pinch off legs of shrimp, several at a time, then bend back and snap off sharp, beaklike piece of shell just above tail. Remove shell and discard. Using sharp paring knife, make shallow incision along back of each shrimp, exposing black digestive vein. Extract black vein and discard. Rinse shrimp under cold running water, drain, and dry with paper towels. Set aside.
7. Reduce heat under poaching liquid in saucepan to medium-high and simmer 15 minutes.
8. Add peas to stockpot and cook 1 to 2 minutes, or until most peas rise to top. Remove peas immediately with large mesh strainer, reserving water in pot, and refresh under cold running water. Transfer peas to small bowl.
9. Return water in stockpot to a boil, add pasta, and cook according to package directions, until just past *al dente*.
10. While pasta is cooking, wash spinach in several changes of cold water; do not dry. Remove and discard tough stems. Cut leaves crosswise into ½-inch-wide strips to measure about 4 cups and place in medium-size skillet.
11. Transfer pasta to colander and set aside to cool.
12. Add shrimp to poaching liquid and cook 5 minutes.
13. Place skillet over medium heat and cook spinach, stirring, 2 minutes, or until spinach is completely wilted. Transfer spinach to large sieve and set aside to cool.
14. Remove shrimp from stockpot with mesh strainer and refresh under cold running water; set aside to cool 15 minutes. Reserve poaching liquid for another use. (If not using within 2 days, freeze in container with lid.)
15. Wash basil and dry with paper towels. Trim off stems and discard. Cut leaves crosswise into ½-inch-wide strips and set aside. You should have ¾ cup packed.
16. Using food processor or grater, grate enough Parmesan to measure ½ cup.
17. When spinach is cool enough to handle, press with back of spoon to remove excess moisture. Transfer to food processor or blender.
18. Add garlic, basil, grated Parmesan, and olive oil to spinach and purée.
19. To assemble salad, combine pasta and peas in large bowl. Add salt and pepper to taste, and toss to combine. Add half the spinach pesto and toss until pasta is evenly coated. Divide among 4 bowls and top with shrimp. Serve with remaining spinach pesto on the side.

Italian Bread with Garlic, Thyme, and Olive Oil

1 long loaf Italian bread
4 cloves garlic, peeled and pressed
2 tablespoons fresh thyme leaves, or 2 teaspoons dried
½ cup olive oil

1. Preheat oven to 450 degrees.
2. Halve bread lengthwise and place on baking sheet, cut sides up.
3. In small bowl, combine garlic, thyme, and olive oil, and stir with fork to combine. Using pastry brush, coat cut sides of bread with oil mixture.
4. Toast bread about 12 minutes, or just until golden.
5. Cut bread on diagonal into 3-inch-wide slices and serve.

Connie Handa Moore

MENU 1 (Right)
Peasant-style Miso Soup
Ham, Vegetable, and Noodle Salad
Strawberries with Frosted Ladyfingers

MENU 2
Shrimp and Vegetable Rice
Japanese Orange Mousse

MENU 3
Glazed Beef and Mushrooms
with Shredded Cabbage
Baked Tomato Pudding

The art of Japanese cooking involves treating all foods with respect—never overcooking them and paying careful attention to the way dishes are presented. "Because we Japanese eat with our eyes," says Connie Handa Moore, "we want our meals to be aesthetically pleasing." Her three Oriental-style salad menus are in keeping with this time-honored tradition.

Menu 1 is a three-course meal that starts with a soup brimming with diced vegetables, tofu, and scallions, and flavored with *miso*. The soup whets the palate for the salad of vegetables, ham, and noodles on crisp spinach leaves. Fresh whole strawberries and ladyfingers frosted with whipped cream and nuts are the tempting dessert.

The beautiful salad of Menu 2 makes a good luncheon or a light dinner. Large shrimp and ribbons of egg crêpe are arranged on a mixture of rice, peas, and *shiitake* mushrooms. The colorful shrimp complement the orange mousse dessert, which can be placed on the table with the main course for visual appeal.

Presentation is again the key in Menu 3. Here strips of beef and mushrooms are stir fried briefly, then placed on a contrasting bed of crisp shredded cabbage coated with a light vinaigrette. Tomato pudding, topped with rings of green bell pepper, is the bright side dish.

The miso *soup garnished with scallions is served in lidded bowls to retain heat. It precedes the ham, vegetable, and noodle salad with strips of cucumber and zucchini, and the light dessert of fresh strawberries with frosted ladyfingers.*

Peasant-style Miso Soup
Ham, Vegetable, and Noodle Salad
Strawberries with Frosted Ladyfingers

Bamboo shoots are a main ingredient in the soup. Most often associated with Chinese cookery, these tender young shoots of tropical bamboo plants have a slightly sweet taste and a crisp texture. They are sold whole or sliced in cans and have the best flavor when packed in water rather than brine.

WHAT TO DRINK

Enjoy a firm, dry white wine with this menu. Sancerre and Pouilly-Fumé would both be excellent, as would their California cousin Sauvignon Blanc.

SHOPPING LIST AND STAPLES

1¼ pounds imported Danish ham
6 ounces firm tofu
Small bunch large-leaf spinach (about ½ pound)
1 pint cherry tomatoes
Large carrot, or small daikon radish (about ¼ pound)
Medium-size cucumber
Medium-size zucchini
Large red onion
Small bunch scallions
Medium-size lemon
1 to 2 pints strawberries, preferably with stems, or raspberries
4 cups chicken stock, preferably homemade (see page 9), or two 10¾-ounce cans condensed chicken broth
8-ounce can bamboo shoots
½ pint heavy cream
1 pound fresh Chinese egg noodles, or ¾ pound dried capellini or spaghettini
½ cup plus 1 tablespoon vegetable oil
½ cup white vinegar
5 tablespoons white miso paste
¾ cup granulated sugar
¼ cup confectioners' sugar
1 package ladyfingers
4-ounce can walnut pieces
Salt
Freshly ground pepper

UTENSILS

Large saucepan or stockpot
Medium-size saucepan with cover

Medium-size bowl
2 small bowls
Colander
Measuring cups and spoons
Chef's knife
Paring knife
Wooden spoon
Rubber spatula
Vegetable brush
Vegetable peeler
Juicer
Electric mixer

START-TO-FINISH STEPS

1. Follow strawberries recipe steps 1 through 5.
2. Follow salad recipe steps 1 through 12.
3. Follow soup recipe steps 1 through 8 and strawberries recipe step 6.
4. Follow soup recipe step 9 and serve as first course.
5. Follow salad recipe step 13 and serve.
6. Follow strawberries recipe step 7 and serve.

RECIPES

Peasant-style Miso Soup

4 cups chicken stock, preferably homemade, or two 10¾-ounce cans condensed chicken broth
Large carrot, or small daikon radish (about ¼ pound)
8-ounce can bamboo shoots
5 tablespoons white miso paste
6 ounces firm tofu
1 scallion

1. Place chicken stock in medium-size saucepan. Or, if using canned chicken broth, skim fat from surface and pour defatted broth plus 2 cans of water into pan. Cover and bring to a boil over medium heat.
2. While stock is heating, peel and trim carrot or daikon. Cut into ¼-inch dice to measure ½ cup.
3. Turn bamboo shoots into colander, rinse under cold running water, and drain. Coarsely chop enough bamboo shoots to measure 1 cup.
4. Add vegetables to stock and return to a boil. Reduce heat, cover, and gently simmer vegetables about 5 minutes, or until crisp-tender.
5. While soup is simmering, measure miso into small

bowl. Add 1 tablespoon hot tap water and stir until thoroughly blended. Set aside.

6. Rinse tofu under cold running water; pat dry with paper towel. Cut tofu into ¼-inch dice; set aside.

7. Rinse scallion and dry with paper towel. Trim ends and discard. Cut on diagonal into ¼-inch slices; set aside.

8. Turn miso into soup and stir until blended. Raise heat to medium-high and bring soup to a boil.

9. As soon as soup comes to a boil, remove pan from heat. Add tofu to soup and divide among individual bowls. Sprinkle with sliced scallion and serve.

Ham, Vegetable, and Noodle Salad

Small bunch large-leaf spinach (about ½ pound)
Large red onion
1 pint cherry tomatoes
Medium-size cucumber
Medium-size zucchini
1¼ pounds imported Danish ham
½ cup plus 1 tablespoon vegetable oil
1 pound fresh Chinese egg noodles, or ¾ pound dried
    capellini or spaghettini
Medium-size lemon
¾ cup granulated sugar
Salt and freshly ground pepper
½ cup white vinegar

1. In large saucepan or stockpot, bring 4 quarts of water to a rapid boil.

2. Meanwhile, remove and discard any bruised or discolored spinach leaves. Wash remaining leaves in several changes of cold water; remove tough stems. Shake leaves and drain in colander; set aside.

3. Peel and halve red onion. Cut into thin slices. Cut slices in half and separate into strips; set aside.

4. Wash and dry cherry tomatoes. Remove stems.

5. Wash and dry cucumber. Trim ends and discard. Halve cucumber crosswise and then halve each piece lengthwise. Cut quarters lengthwise into ¼-inch julienne.

6. Under cold running water, scrub zucchini with vegetable brush to remove sand; dry with paper towel. Cut zucchini into ¼-inch julienne; set aside.

7. Cut ham into ¼-inch julienne; set aside.

8. Add 1 tablespoon oil to boiling water to prevent noodles from sticking together. Add noodles, stir with wooden spoon to separate, and cook 2 to 3 minutes for fresh, or according to package directions for dried.

9. Squeeze lemon to measure 2 tablespoons juice.

10. Turn noodles into colander and rinse under cold running water; set aside to drain.

11. For dressing, combine sugar, 2 teaspoons salt, ½ teaspoon pepper, vinegar, lemon juice, and ½ cup oil in small bowl and beat with fork until blended; set aside.

12. Divide spinach among 4 dinner plates. Divide noodles among plates, mounding them in center. Top noodles with cucumber, zucchini, and onion. Arrange cherry tomatoes and ham strips decoratively around noodles; cover and set aside until ready to serve.

13. Just before serving, stir dressing to recombine and serve with salads.

Strawberries with Frosted Ladyfingers

1 to 2 pints strawberries, preferably with stems,
    or raspberries
¼ to ½ cup walnut pieces
½ pint heavy cream
4 to 8 ladyfingers
¼ cup confectioners' sugar

1. Place medium-size bowl and beaters for whipping cream in freezer to chill.

2. Leave stems on strawberries and gently rinse berries under cold running water. Transfer to double thickness of paper towels and pat dry. Divide berries among 4 dessert plates; set aside.

3. Coarsely chop walnuts; set aside.

4. Pour cream into chilled bowl. Using electric mixer, whip cream until soft peaks form.

5. Separate ladyfingers into single sections and spread each half with a layer of whipped cream. Sprinkle with walnuts and divide ladyfingers among plates with berries. Cover each serving with plastic wrap and refrigerate.

6. Twenty minutes before serving, remove plates from refrigerator.

7. When ready to serve, place confectioners' sugar in small bowl and serve separately with strawberries and ladyfingers.

ADDED TOUCH

For an impressive appetizer or *hors d'oeuvre*, sculpture cucumber sections into attractive cups to hold slices of smoked salmon.

Cucumber Cups with Gravlax and Capers

1 head Bibb lettuce
Small lemon
1 large English hothouse cucumber (about 16 inches long)
12 thin slices gravlax or Nova lox
4 teaspoons capers, rinsed and drained

1. Wash and dry lettuce. Remove any bruised or discolored leaves. Divide among 4 salad plates; set aside.

2. Wash and dry lemon. Cut crosswise into four ¼-inch-thick slices; set aside.

3. Wash and dry cucumber. Trim ends and discard. With sharp paring knife, cut cucumber crosswise into approximately 4-inch quarters. Cut 1-inch-deep triangles around one end of each quarter to form crown shape. Using melon baller or teaspoon, scoop out inside, leaving ¼ inch of flesh at bottom, to form cup for filling.

4. Stuff each cucumber cup with two slices of gravlax and top with 1 teaspoon capers.

5. Divide cucumber cups among lettuce-lined plates. Fold remaining slices of gravlax into cone shape and place one next to each cucumber cup. Garnish each plate with a lemon slice and serve.

Shrimp and Vegetable Rice
Japanese Orange Mousse

Golden ribbons of egg garnish this beautifully composed salad of shrimp, vegetables, and rice. The dessert is orange mousse.

Thin, delicate ribbons of egg make an unusual topping for the shrimp and vegetable rice salad. Before cooking, lightly grease the skillet with oil, heat the skillet, then slowly pour in just enough beaten egg mixture to form a paper-thin sheet. As you pour, rotate the hot skillet so the egg is evenly distributed. Do not allow the egg to brown; the finished egg strips should be pale yellow. Slice the cooked egg thinly—the thinner the slices, the more delicate they appear. You can vary the salad by substituting drained canned white-meat tuna or poached chicken slices for the cooked shrimp.

The foamy orange mousse is garnished with Mandarin orange, whipped cream, mint leaves, and slivers of crystallized ginger. Mandarin oranges originated in China and are similar to tangerines, which can be substituted. Crystallized, or candied, ginger is covered with sugar, so use it sparingly or the dessert will be too sweet.

WHAT TO DRINK

The cook recommends a fruity white wine with a touch of sweetness: Vouvray is the first choice, or try California Chenin Blanc or German Riesling.

SHOPPING LIST AND STAPLES

1¼ pounds large shrimp
Medium-size carrot
Small bunch mint
11-ounce can Mandarin oranges
8-ounce can whole water chestnuts
1 egg
½ pint heavy cream
1 pint vanilla ice cream
10-ounce package frozen peas
5 tablespoons white vinegar
⅓ cup mayonnaise, preferably homemade (see page 12)
1 tablespoon ketchup
2 teaspoons Japanese soy sauce
Hot pepper sauce
2 cups long-grain rice
8 dried shiitake mushrooms (about ¼ pound total weight), or ½ pound fresh button mushrooms
4-ounce can walnuts or almonds
Two 3-ounce packages orange-flavored gelatin
4¼-ounce package crystallized ginger
½ cup plus ½ teaspoon sugar
Salt
1 teaspoon dry white wine
2 tablespoons orange-flavored liqueur

UTENSILS

Large nonstick skillet
Stockpot or large saucepan
Medium-size heavy-gauge saucepan with cover
Small saucepan
2 large bowls

Medium-size bowl
4 small bowls
Colander
Large strainer
Measuring cups and spoons
Chef's knife
Paring knife
2 wooden spoons
Rubber spatula
Whisk
Vegetable peeler
Electric mixer

START-TO-FINISH STEPS

One hour ahead: Set out frozen peas to thaw at room temperature.

Thirty minutes ahead: Remove vanilla ice cream from freezer and set out until it has a semi-soft but still firm consistency.

1. Follow mousse recipe steps 1 through 8.
2. Follow rice recipe steps 1 through 20 and serve with mousse.

RECIPES

Shrimp and Vegetable Rice

2 cups long-grain rice
3 teaspoons salt
1¼ pounds large shrimp
8 dried shiitake mushrooms (about ¼ pound total weight), or ½ pound fresh button mushrooms
½ cup plus ½ teaspoon sugar
Medium-size carrot
8-ounce can whole water chestnuts
10-ounce package frozen peas, thawed
1 egg
¼ cup walnuts or almonds
5 tablespoons white vinegar
1 teaspoon dry white wine
⅓ cup mayonnaise
2 teaspoons Japanese soy sauce
1 tablespoon ketchup
Hot pepper sauce

1. In medium-size heavy-gauge saucepan, bring 3½ cups of water to a rapid boil over high heat. Add rice and 1 teaspoon salt, return to a boil, and stir rice with wooden spoon. Cover pan, reduce heat, and simmer 20 minutes.
2. While rice simmers, bring 4 quarts of water to a rapid boil in stockpot over high heat.
3. While water is heating, peel and devein shrimp (see following illustration): Pinch off legs of shrimp, several at a time, then bend back and snap off sharp, beaklike piece of shell just above tail. Remove shell and discard. Using sharp paring knife, make shallow incision along back of each shrimp, exposing black digestive vein. Extract black

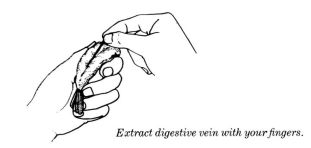

Pinch off legs to remove shell.

Extract digestive vein with your fingers.

vein with your fingers and discard. Place shrimp in colander, rinse under cold running water, and drain.

4. Add shrimp to boiling water in stockpot and cook 3 to 4 minutes, or until backs of shrimp turn opaque and begin to curl.

5. Fluff rice with fork and turn into large bowl; set aside to cool. Rinse saucepan.

6. Turn shrimp into colander and refresh under cold running water; set aside to cool.

7. Bring 3 cups of water to a boil in medium-size saucepan over high heat. If using button mushrooms, wipe clean with damp paper towels; leave whole. Add ¼ cup sugar, 1 teaspoon salt, and shiitake or button mushrooms to boiling water and stir. When water returns to a boil, cover pan, reduce heat, and simmer 15 minutes for shiitake or 5 minutes for button mushrooms.

8. While mushrooms are simmering, bring 1 cup of water to a boil in small saucepan over medium-high heat.

9. Meanwhile, peel and trim carrot. Halve crosswise and then halve each piece lengthwise. Cut quarters into 1-inch-long slivers. You should have about ¾ cup.

10. Add carrot to boiling water and blanch 1 minute. Turn into large strainer and refresh under cold running water. Transfer to small plate and set aside to cool.

11. Turn water chestnuts into strainer and rinse under cold running water; dry with paper towels. Cut into ⅛-inch-thick slices; set aside.

12. Turn thawed peas into strainer and drain. Transfer to small bowl and set aside.

13. Turn mushrooms into strainer and rinse under cold running water; drain. Transfer mushrooms to double thickness of paper towels and press to remove excess moisture. Remove and discard stems of shiitake and cut caps into ⅛-inch-thick slices; if using button mushrooms, leave whole. Set mushrooms aside.

14. Using paper towel that has been dipped in oil, grease large nonstick skillet and heat over medium-high heat until hot.

15. Meanwhile, crack egg into small bowl. Add ½ teaspoon sugar and 1 teaspoon water, and whisk until blended. Slowly pour just enough egg into pan to barely coat bottom and cook about 1 minute or until crêpe appears dry; do *not* allow to brown. When set, loosen edge of crêpe with rubber spatula and flip over onto clean work surface. Regrease pan, beat egg to recombine, and repeat until all egg mixture is used.

16. Stack crêpes and roll stack into cylinder. Using a sharp knife, cut crosswise into very thin strips. Transfer strips to a plate and toss to separate; set aside.

17. Coarsely chop walnuts; set aside.

18. For vinaigrette, combine white vinegar, ¼ cup sugar, 1 teaspoon salt, and white wine in small bowl and whisk until blended.

19. Combine mayonnaise, soy sauce, ketchup, and dash of hot pepper sauce in a small bowl and stir until blended. Turn into serving dish and set aside.

20. Add mushrooms, carrots, water chestnuts, and vinaigrette to rice and stir with wooden spoon to combine. Divide mixture among 4 dinner plates and sprinkle with drained peas. Top with equal portions of egg strips and arrange shrimp around border of each plate. Sprinkle with nuts and serve with spicy mayonnaise on the side.

Japanese Orange Mousse

Small bunch mint
⅓ cup crystallized ginger
11-ounce can Mandarin oranges
Two 3-ounce packages orange-flavored gelatin
2 tablespoons orange-flavored liqueur
1 pint vanilla ice cream, semi-soft
½ cup heavy cream

1. Place medium-size bowl and beaters for whipping cream in freezer to chill.

2. Rinse mint and dry with paper towels. Set aside 12 leaves for garnish; refrigerate remainder for another use.

3. Slice ginger into thin slivers; set aside.

4. Drain Mandarin oranges; set aside.

5. In small saucepan, bring 1 cup of water to a boil over high heat. Add orange-flavored gelatin and stir with wooden spoon until thoroughly dissolved.

6. Pour gelatin mixture into large bowl, add 3 ice cubes and liqueur, and stir until ice melts. Add ice cream and whisk by hand until light and fluffy. Cover mixture with plastic wrap and place in freezer.

7. Pour heavy cream into chilled bowl and beat with electric mixer until cream stands in soft peaks.

8. Divide mousse among 4 serving bowls or goblets and top each serving with a spoonful of whipped cream. Arrange orange slices and mint leaves decoratively around whipped cream. Garnish whipped cream with ginger slices. Cover desserts with plastic wrap and refrigerate until ready to serve.

Glazed Beef and Mushrooms
with Shredded Cabbage
Baked Tomato Pudding

For a quick family meal, serve beef and mushrooms on a bed of shredded cabbage coated with vinaigrette dressing. Baked tomato pudding garnished with green pepper rings is the vegetable side dish.

The stir-fried beef strips are glazed with a sauce seasoned with *mirin*, a sweet rice wine that is frequently used in Japanese cooking. Once opened, *mirin* lasts for several months on a pantry shelf and indefinitely in the refrigerator. If you cannot locate it in a specialty food store, you can make your own by combining equal parts sherry and sugar, then cooking the mixture over low heat until syrupy.

WHAT TO DRINK

The spiciness of a well-chilled California Gerwürztraminer would enhance the varied flavors of this meal. An Alsatian or Italian Gewürztraminer is also good.

SHOPPING LIST AND STAPLES

1¼ to 1½ pounds boneless sirloin or other lean beef, cut into 2-inch-wide strips
8 medium-size mushrooms (about 6 ounces total weight)
Small head Chinese or Savoy cabbage (about 1 pound)
1 Italian green pepper
Small onion
Small bunch scallions
Large clove garlic
2-inch piece fresh ginger
Small bunch fresh basil, or 1 tablespoon dried
Small bunch fresh coriander for garnish (optional)
28-ounce can crushed tomatoes
2 tablespoons unsalted butter, approximately
9 tablespoons plus 1 teaspoon vegetable oil
¼ cup white vinegar
¼ cup Japanese soy sauce
16-ounce can large pitted black olives
1 slice firm white bread
2 tablespoons unseasoned bread crumbs
½ cup plus 2 tablespoons sugar
1 tablespoon cornstarch
2½-ounce jar sesame seeds
Salt
Freshly ground white and black pepper
2 tablespoons mirin

UTENSILS

Food processor (optional)
Large heavy-gauge skillet

Medium-size skillet
Small heavy-gauge skillet
Large bowl
Medium-size bowl
2 small bowls
Colander
Measuring cups and spoons
Chef's knife
Paring knife
Wooden spoon
Slotted spoon
Rubber spatula

START-TO-FINISH STEPS

1. Follow tomato pudding recipe steps 1 through 9.
2. While tomato pudding is baking, follow salad recipe steps 1 through 15.
3. Follow tomato pudding recipe step 10 and salad recipe steps 16 through 18.
4. Follow tomato pudding recipe steps 11 and 12, and serve with salad.

RECIPES

Glazed Beef and Mushrooms with Shredded Cabbage

2 tablespoons sesame seeds
¼ cup plus 3 tablespoons sugar
½ cup plus 1 tablespoon vegetable oil
¼ cup white vinegar
1 teaspoon salt
½ teaspoon freshly ground black pepper
Small bunch fresh coriander for garnish (optional)
Small head Chinese or Savoy cabbage (about 1 pound)
8 medium-size mushrooms (about 6 ounces total weight)
2 scallions
2-inch piece fresh ginger
Large clove garlic
1 tablespoon cornstarch
¼ cup Japanese soy sauce
2 tablespoons mirin
1¼ to 1½ pounds boneless sirloin or other lean beef, cut into 2-inch-wide strips
16-ounce can large pitted black olives

1. In small heavy-gauge skillet, toast sesame seeds over medium heat, shaking skillet to prevent scorching. When seeds start to pop, remove skillet from heat. Set aside.
2. For vinaigrette, combine 3 tablespoons sugar, ½ cup oil, vinegar, salt, and pepper in small bowl and beat with fork until blended; set aside.
3. Wash coriander, if using, and dry with paper towels. Trim off root ends, leaving 2-inch-long sprigs. Wrap in paper towels and refrigerate until ready to serve.
4. Wash cabbage and dry with paper towels. Quarter cabbage; remove and discard core. Using food processor fitted with slicing disk, feed each quarter into tube, with core side at right angle to disk, and pulse until all cabbage is sliced. Or, thinly slice each quarter with chef's knife.
5. Place cabbage in large bowl and add enough ice water to cover; set aside.

Chinese cabbage

6. Wipe mushrooms clean with damp paper towels. Remove and discard stems. Cut caps into ⅛-inch-thick slices; set aside.
7. Wash scallions and dry with paper towels. Trim ends and discard. Thinly slice scallions; set aside.
8. Grate enough ginger to measure 2 teaspoons; set aside.

Fresh ginger

9. Peel and mince garlic; set aside.
10. Combine cornstarch, soy sauce, remaining sugar, mirin, and ginger in small bowl and stir to combine. Pour into medium-size skillet and heat over medium heat, stirring constantly with a wooden spoon, 1 to 2 minutes, or until sauce thickens and starts to bubble. Remove skillet from heat and set aside.
11. Transfer cabbage to colander and shake to drain as much water as possible. Dry large bowl. Return cabbage to bowl, cover with plastic wrap, and refrigerate.

12. Heat 1 tablespoon oil in large heavy-gauge skillet over high heat for 30 seconds. Reduce heat to medium-low, add garlic and scallions, and stir 1 minute. With slotted spoon, transfer garlic and scallions to measuring cup; set aside.
13. Using same skillet, quickly stir fry meat over medium-high heat about 3 minutes, or until it loses its pink color.
14. Add mushrooms to meat and cook another 30 seconds. Transfer meat and mushrooms to colander and drain.
15. Return meat and mushrooms to skillet, add sautéed scallions and garlic and sauce, and stir to combine. Remove pan from heat and set aside.
16. Drain olives; set aside.
17. Stir dressing to recombine. Remove cabbage from refrigerator, add dressing, and toss until evenly coated.
18. Divide cabbage among 4 dinner plates, making well in center of cabbage. Spoon meat and mushroom mixture into wells. Sprinkle cabbage with toasted sesame seeds. Garnish each serving with large black olives and sprigs of coriander, if desired.

Baked Tomato Pudding

1 teaspoon vegetable oil
28-ounce can crushed tomatoes
Small onion
Large fresh basil leaf, or 1 tablespoon dried
5 teaspoons unsalted butter
1 slice firm white bread
3 tablespoons sugar
Salt and freshly ground white pepper
2 tablespoons unseasoned bread crumbs
1 Italian green pepper for garnish

1. Preheat oven to 350 degrees. Set rack in top half of oven.
2. Grease four 1½-cup ramekins or ovenproof dishes with vegetable oil.
3. Pour tomatoes into medium-size bowl.
4. Peel and finely chop enough onion to measure ⅓ cup. Wash basil leaf, if using, and chop finely.
5. Melt 1 teaspoon butter in small heavy-gauge skillet over medium heat. Add onion and basil, and sauté, stirring occasionally, 3 to 5 minutes, or until onion is soft and translucent.
6. While onion is sautéing, cut bread slice into ½-inch cubes and add to tomatoes.
7. Add onion and basil mixture, sugar, salt, and a pinch of pepper to tomatoes; stir to combine. Rinse and dry skillet.

8. Divide tomato pudding mixture among prepared ramekins or dishes, leveling tops with spatula. Sprinkle bread crumbs lightly over puddings and dot each serving with 1 teaspoon of remaining butter.
9. Reduce oven temperature to 325 degrees and bake puddings in top half of oven 30 minutes.
10. Turn off heat and keep warm in oven until ready to serve.
11. Just before serving, wash pepper and dry with paper towel. Slice pepper into ⅛-inch-thick rings; remove and discard ribs and seeds.
12. Remove puddings from oven, garnish with pepper rings, and serve.

ADDED TOUCH

Soba noodles (see page 10), snow peas, and scallions flavored with soy sauce and sesame oil make a substantial accompaniment for this salad.

Soba Noodles with Snow Peas and Scallions

¼ pound snow peas
3 scallions
10-ounce package soba noodles
3 tablespoons soy sauce
3 teaspoons sesame oil

1. Bring 3 quarts of water to a boil in stockpot over high heat. Bring 2 cups of water to a boil in small saucepan over medium-high heat.
2. Rinse snow peas under cold running water. Remove and discard strings. Add peas to small saucepan of boiling water. When water returns to a boil, turn peas into strainer and refresh under cold running water; set aside.
3. Wash and dry scallions. Trim ends and discard. Cut scallions crosswise into ¼-inch-thick slices; set aside.
4. Add noodles to stockpot of boiling water and stir with wooden spoon to separate. Cover pot to help water return to a boil; then remove cover and continue cooking noodles 6 minutes, stirring occasionally.
5. Turn noodles into colander and rinse under hot running water for 30 seconds to remove starch.
6. Turn noodles into large mixing bowl, add soy sauce and sesame oil, and toss until evenly coated.
7. Divide noodles among 4 plates, sprinkle with scallions and snow peas, and serve.

Susan Huberman

A s a professional food stylist, Susan Huberman must make every dish she prepares look appealing, so she is particularly conscious of how the colors, shapes, and textures of foods work together. Naturally, when cooking at home, she is aware of the same things, but she is also wary of fixing overly arranged dishes that might intimidate her guests. "I want people to dig in and enjoy my food," she says. "No one should be afraid to eat a meal because it appears too elaborate." The three salad menus offered here are not only inviting but also taste as good as they look.

Menus 1 and 3 are for occasions when you want to impress special friends. The cook describes Menu 1 as a sensual dinner because it is especially pleasing to the palate. There is the luxury of caviar in the first course, followed by fresh crabmeat and wild mushrooms, and a crisp salad of mâche (lamb's lettuce), romaine, jícama, and red cabbage. Menu 3 consists of three very different but elegant salads: warm duck with mango chutney, rice with pecans and mint, and sliced oranges and radishes spiced with cinnamon dressing.

Menu 2 is a colorful Italian meal, ideal for late summer when peppers and basil abound. Susan Huberman roasts the peppers and combines them with sun-dried tomatoes, mozzarella, basil leaves, and vinaigrette. With this she offers fresh pasta tossed with vegetables and Genoa salami, and a mixed green salad with pears.

A selection of fresh vegetables with a caviar dip makes an excellent cocktail-hour hors d'oeuvre or a perfect first course. Follow this with crabmeat and wild mushrooms, and mâche and romaine lettuce with garlic-ginger vinaigrette.

Crudités with Caviar Dip
Crabmeat and Wild Mushroom Salad
Mixed Greens with Jícama and Red Cabbage

Strictly speaking, caviar is the roe of the sturgeon, but the generic term includes the roe of other fish as well, such as the lumpfish. Lumpfish caviar, used here in the dip, is not expensive and adds instant elegance to any menu. If stored in a cool, dark place, an unopened can or jar of this caviar will keep for several months; once opened, it keeps for about a week in the refrigerator.

The accompanying tossed salad calls for jícama, a vegetable native to Mexico that is usually eaten raw. Shaped like a large turnip, jícama has a taste and texture similar to a water chestnut's. It can be found in West Coast supermarkets; elsewhere, look for it at greengrocers and Mexican markets. Store jícama in the refrigerator in a plastic bag or sliced and immersed in water in a covered container. Jerusalem artichokes or a large black radish are a substitute.

WHAT TO DRINK

A dry white wine is called for here. For full body and fruitiness, choose a California Chardonnay; for crispness, an Italian Pinot Grigio or Pinot Bianco; for delicacy and charm, a Moselle Riesling.

SHOPPING LIST AND STAPLES

1 pound fresh or frozen crabmeat
Small head red cabbage (about 1 pound)
1 pound whole white baby turnips
Small jícama (about ½ pound), or ½ pound Jerusalem artichokes
2 small yellow squash (about ½ pound total weight)
Small yellow or white onion
1 bunch baby carrots
2 heads Bibb lettuce
1 head romaine lettuce
1 bunch mâche, or 1 head Boston lettuce
Medium-size red bell pepper
1 pint cherry tomatoes
1 bunch scallions
1 bunch red radishes
4 to 6 shallots
1 clove garlic
¼ pound fresh shiitake, oyster, morel, or chanterelle mushrooms
Small bunch fresh coriander or parsley
2-inch piece fresh ginger

2 limes
½ pint sour cream
8-ounce container whipped cream cheese
2-ounce jar red lumpfish caviar
⅓ cup olive oil, approximately
¼ cup vegetable oil
¾ cup mayonnaise, preferably homemade (see page 12), or prepared
¼ cup rice wine vinegar
Salt and freshly ground pepper

UTENSILS

Food processor or blender
Small skillet or sauté pan
Large bowl
Medium-size bowl
Small bowl
Measuring cups and spoons
Chef's knife
Paring knife
Wooden spoon
Slotted spoon
Rubber spatula
Whisk
Vegetable peeler
Garlic press
Juicer
Grater

START-TO-FINISH STEPS

One hour ahead: If using frozen crabmeat, immerse in cold water to thaw.

1. Wash lettuce for all three recipes and dry. Remove and discard any bruised or discolored leaves. Wrap Bibb lettuce in paper towels for crabmeat and mushroom salad recipe and refrigerate until ready to serve.
2. Follow crudités recipe steps 1 through 6.
3. Follow crabmeat and mushroom salad recipe steps 1 through 6.
4. While mushrooms are cooking, follow mixed salad recipe steps 1 through 5.
5. Follow crabmeat and mushroom salad recipe steps 7 through 11.
6. Follow mixed salad recipe steps 6 through 8.
7. Follow crudités recipe step 7 and serve as first course.

8. Follow crabmeat and mushroom salad recipe step 12, mixed salad recipe step 9, and serve on same plate, if desired.

RECIPES

Crudités with Caviar Dip

Small yellow or white onion
½ cup whipped cream cheese
½ cup sour cream
¼ cup red lumpfish caviar
1 bunch scallions
1 bunch red radishes
1 bunch baby carrots
1 pound whole white baby turnips
2 small yellow squash (about ½ pound total weight)
Medium-size red bell pepper
7 or 8 outer leaves romaine lettuce

1. Halve and peel onion. Finely chop enough to measure 2 tablespoons; reserve remainder for another use.
2. Using food processor or blender, process cream cheese about 30 seconds, or until smooth. Add sour cream and process until well blended. Add onion and process just until combined. Turn mixture into small serving bowl.
3. If necessary, drain caviar; then gently fold into dip, reserving ½ teaspoon for garnish; cover and set aside.
4. Trim scallions, radishes, carrots, turnips, and squash. Wash and dry with paper towels. Peel carrots and turnips. Cut squash on diagonal into ¼-inch-thick slices. Set vegetables aside.
5. Wash and dry red bell pepper. Halve, core, and seed pepper; cut lengthwise into ½-inch-wide strips.
6. Line serving platter with romaine leaves. Place bowl of dip on platter and arrange vegetables decoratively around it. Cover with plastic wrap and refrigerate until ready to serve.
7. Just before serving, sprinkle dip with reserved caviar.

Crabmeat and Wild Mushroom Salad

1 pound fresh or frozen crabmeat
¼ pound fresh shiitake, oyster, morel, or
 chanterelle mushrooms
4 to 6 shallots
⅓ cup olive oil, approximately
2 limes
Salt
Freshly ground pepper
Small bunch fresh coriander or parsley
½ pint cherry tomatoes
2 heads Bibb lettuce

1. Place crabmeat in medium-size bowl. Remove any cartilage or bits of shell and discard. Flake crabmeat with fork; set aside.
2. Wipe mushrooms with damp paper towels. Cut off stem ends and discard. Cut mushrooms into ¼-inch-thick slices and set aside.

3. Peel and coarsely chop enough shallots to measure 3 tablespoons.
4. In small skillet or sauté pan, heat olive oil over medium heat. Add shallots and sauté, stirring occasionally, 3 minutes, or until soft.
5. Meanwhile, squeeze enough lime juice to measure ¼ cup; set aside.
6. Add mushrooms to skillet and sauté, stirring occasionally, another 10 minutes.
7. With slotted spoon, transfer mushrooms to bowl with crabmeat. Reserve oil in pan.
8. For dressing, if necessary, add enough oil to reserved oil in skillet to measure ½ cup. Add lime juice and salt and pepper to taste, and whisk until blended; set aside.
9. Wash coriander or parsley and dry with paper towels. Chop enough to measure ¼ cup; add to crabmeat. Reserve remainder for another use.
10. Wash and dry cherry tomatoes; remove and discard stems. Halve tomatoes; add to bowl with crabmeat.
11. Whisk dressing to recombine and pour over salad; toss until salad ingredients are evenly coated. Cover with plastic wrap and refrigerate until ready to serve.
12. Divide lettuce among 4 dinner plates and top with equal portions of salad.

Mixed Greens with Jícama and Red Cabbage

¾ cup mayonnaise
1 clove garlic
2-inch piece fresh ginger
¼ cup vegetable oil
¼ cup rice wine vinegar
Salt and freshly ground pepper
3 or 4 inner leaves romaine lettuce
1 bunch mâche, or 1 head Boston lettuce
Small head red cabbage (about 1 pound)
Small jícama (about ½ pound), or ½ pound Jerusalem
 artichokes

1. Turn mayonnaise into small bowl and stir until creamy.
2. Peel garlic and put through press into mayonnaise.
3. Peel and grate enough fresh ginger to measure 2 tablespoons. Add to mayonnaise and stir with fork to blend.
4. Beating with fork, slowly add vegetable oil to mayonnaise and stir until blended.
5. Add vinegar, and salt and pepper to taste, and stir to combine. Cover and refrigerate until ready to serve.
6. Break lettuce and mâche into bite-size pieces and place in large bowl.
7. Wash and dry cabbage; halve and core. Cut enough cabbage crosswise into ⅛-inch-wide strips to measure about 1½ cups; reserve remainder for another use. Add cabbage to bowl.
8. Peel jícama or Jerusalem artichokes and cut enough into ⅛-inch-thick slices to measure 1 cup. Reserve remainder for another use. Add to bowl, cover, and refrigerate.
9. Just before serving, pour dressing over salad and toss until evenly coated.

Roasted Peppers with Mozzarella and Sun-Dried Tomatoes
Pasta and Vegetables with Genoa Salami
Pear, Arugula, and Belgian Endive Salad

For a particularly dazzling presentation, serve all three of these Italian salads on the same plate.

Mild mozzarella cheese is delicious with *pumate* (Italian sun-dried tomatoes with a highly concentrated flavor) and red, green, and yellow roasted peppers. *Pumate* are sold dried or oil packed at specialty food shops and Italian groceries. Although they are expensive, these tomatoes are well worth serving as a special treat. There are no substitutes.

Fresh *fusilli* (corkscrew pasta) tastes best in the salad, but you can use packaged dried *fusilli* if fresh is unavailable. This salad can be prepared the night before you plan to serve it, but be sure the pasta is cooked *al dente*, or it will get soggy in the dressing.

WHAT TO DRINK

A young Italian Chianti, Dolcetto, or Barbera would be good here. Or, if you prefer a domestic wine, consider a young California Gamay Beaujolais.

SHOPPING LIST AND STAPLES

2 ounces thinly sliced Genoa salami (about 6 slices)
2 each red, green, and yellow bell peppers, or any combination
2 medium-size carrots (about ½ pound total weight)

68

Medium-size zucchini
1 bunch arugula
2 heads Belgian endive
Small bunch scallions
4 cloves garlic
1 bunch fresh basil, or 1 tablespoon dried
1 lemon
2 firm pears, such as Bosc
1 egg
½ pound fresh mozzarella cheese, or 8-ounce package good-quality mozzarella
10-ounce package frozen green peas
2½ cups good-quality olive oil
1 cup red wine vinegar, approximately
⅓ cup Dijon mustard
¼ pound sun-dried tomatoes
6-ounce jar whole pimientos
6-ounce can pitted black olives
¼ pound fresh or dried green fusilli
¼ pound fresh or dried white fusilli
Salt and freshly ground pepper

UTENSILS

Blender or food processor
Large saucepan
Medium-size saucepan with cover
Broiler pan with rack
Large shallow dish
Large bowl
Medium-size bowl
3 small bowls
Vegetable steamer
Colander
Strainer
Measuring cups and spoons
Chef's knife
Paring knife
2 wooden spoons
Metal tongs
Vegetable peeler
Brown paper bag

START-TO-FINISH STEPS

1. Peel and coarsely chop garlic for peppers recipe and pear salad recipe.
2. Follow pasta salad recipe steps 1 through 6.
3. While vegetables are steaming, follow peppers recipe steps 1 through 3.
4. While peppers are broiling, follow pasta salad recipe steps 7 through 11.
5. Follow peppers recipe step 4.
6. While peppers are steaming, follow pasta salad recipe steps 12 through 15.
7. Follow peppers recipe steps 5 through 9.
8. Follow pear salad recipe steps 1 through 7, pasta salad recipe step 16, peppers recipe step 10, and serve.

Roasted Peppers with Mozzarella and Sun-Dried Tomatoes

2 each red, green, and yellow bell peppers, or any combination
½ pound fresh mozzarella cheese, or 8-ounce package good-quality mozzarella
1 bunch fresh basil, or 1 tablespoon dried
¼ cup good-quality olive oil
2 tablespoons red wine vinegar
2 cloves garlic, coarsely chopped
¼ pound sun-dried tomatoes

1. Set broiler pan 4 inches from heating element and preheat broiler.
2. Wash and dry peppers. Halve, core, and seed.
3. Arrange peppers, skin-side up, on rack in broiler pan. Broil peppers 10 minutes, or until skins are blackened.
4. Using metal tongs, transfer peppers to brown paper bag, close bag, and set peppers aside to steam about 10 minutes.
5. Remove peppers from paper bag. Holding each half under cold running water, gently rub off blackened skin; dry with paper towels.
6. Cut cheese into ¼-inch-thick slices.
7. Wash fresh basil, if using, and dry with paper towels. Strip leaves from stems; discard stems.
8. In small bowl, combine oil, vinegar, garlic, and dried basil if using, and beat with fork until blended.
9. Pour half the dressing into large shallow dish. Add peppers and cheese slices, overlapping and alternating slices of each. Top with fresh basil leaves if using, and tomatoes and drizzle with remaining dressing, if desired. Set aside until ready to serve.
10. Divide peppers and cheese among dinner plates.

Pasta and Vegetables with Genoa Salami

Medium-size zucchini
Small bunch scallions
2 medium-size carrots (about ½ pound total weight)
1 cup frozen green peas
6-ounce can pitted black olives
¼ cup good-quality olive oil
2 tablespoons red wine vinegar
Salt and freshly ground pepper
¼ pound fresh or dried green fusilli
¼ pound fresh or dried white fusilli
6-ounce jar whole pimientos
2 ounces thinly sliced Genoa salami (about 6 slices)

1. Wash zucchini and scallions, and dry with paper towels. Trim off ends and discard. Cut zucchini crosswise into ¼-inch-thick rounds; set aside. You should have about 1 cup. Thinly slice enough scallions to measure ¼ cup; reserve remaining scallions for another use.
2. Peel and trim carrots. Cut crosswise into ¼-inch-thick slices to measure about 1 cup.

3. Fit medium-size saucepan with vegetable steamer and fill pan with enough water to come up to but not above bottom of steamer. Bring water to a boil over medium-high heat.

4. Place peas in small bowl of cold water to thaw.

5. Add carrots and zucchini to pan, cover, and steam about 5 minutes, or until zucchini is just tender when pierced with tip of a knife and carrots are still crisp.

6. Meanwhile, in large saucepan, bring 3 quarts of water to a boil over high heat.

7. Transfer steamed vegetables to large bowl.

8. Drain peas and add to vegetables.

9. Drain olives, halve lengthwise, and add to vegetables.

10. Combine olive oil, vinegar, and salt and pepper to taste in small bowl, and beat with fork until blended. Add to vegetables and toss until evenly coated.

11. Add 1 tablespoon salt and the pasta to boiling water, and cook, stirring frequently, 2 to 3 minutes for fresh pasta, 8 to 12 minutes for dried, or until *al dente*.

12. Turn pasta into colander to drain. Add warm pasta to vegetable mixture and toss gently to combine. Set aside to cool to room temperature, tossing mixture occasionally.

13. Rinse pimientos under cold running water and dry. Cut lengthwise into ⅛-inch-wide strips.

14. Stack salami slices and cut into ⅛-inch-wide strips.

15. When pasta has cooled, add pimientos and salami to bowl, and toss to combine. Adjust balance of oil and vinegar, and correct seasoning, if necessary. Cover salad with plastic wrap and refrigerate until ready to serve.

16. Just before serving, remove salad from refrigerator and toss to recombine. Divide salad among dinner plates.

Pear, Arugula, and Belgian Endive Salad

1 bunch arugula
2 heads Belgian endive
1 lemon
2 firm pears, such as Bosc
1 egg
⅓ cup Dijon mustard
⅔ cup red wine vinegar
2 cloves garlic, coarsely chopped
2 cups good-quality olive oil
Salt and freshly ground pepper

1. Wash arugula thoroughly and dry with paper towels. Break into bite-size pieces; set aside.

2. Rinse and dry endive. Trim off stem ends and discard. Cut endive crosswise into ½-inch-wide pieces; set aside.

3. Halve lemon and squeeze 1 tablespoon juice into medium-size bowl. Reserve remaining half lemon for another use. Add cold water to fill bowl two-thirds full.

4. Peel and halve pears lengthwise; core. Cut each half lengthwise into ¼-inch-thick slices. Place pear slices in bowl with lemon water to prevent discoloration; set aside.

5. For dressing, combine egg, mustard, vinegar, and garlic in blender or food processor. With machine running, add olive oil in a slow, steady stream and process until dressing is thick and smooth. Add salt and pepper to taste and process dressing just until blended.

6. Drain pears and dry with paper towels.

7. Divide arugula and endive among 4 dinner plates and top with pear slices. Spoon some dressing over each salad and serve remaining dressing on the side, if desired.

ADDED TOUCH

This luxurious dessert is like a frozen chocolate truffle, hence its name, *gelato di tartufo*, or ice cream truffle.

Gelato di Tartufo

6-ounce package semisweet chocolate pieces
1 pint chocolate ice cream
4 pieces candied chocolate cherries, or 7-ounce package marzipan

1. Place chocolate in heatproof measuring cup and place cup in small saucepan.

2. Fill saucepan with enough hot tap water to reach two-thirds of the way up the cup. Allow chocolate to melt slowly, stirring occasionally. A candy thermometer should register 96 to 98 degrees for perfect consistency, or the chocolate should feel just warm, not hot, to your finger.

3. While chocolate is melting, remove ice cream from freezer and set aside about 10 minutes to soften.

4. Meanwhile, if using marzipan, break off four 1-inch pieces and roll between your palms to form balls.

5. Place 1 candied cherry or 1 marzipan ball in center of ice cream scoop. Fill scoop with ice cream so that the candy is buried in the center. Transfer ice cream to serving dish and place in freezer. Repeat process for remaining candies.

6. When all four servings are in freezer, one at a time remove from freezer, drizzle evenly with one-quarter of melted chocolate, and return to freezer.

7. About 10 minutes before serving, remove desserts from freezer.

Warm Duck Salad with Mango Chutney
Rice with Pecans and Mint
Orange and Radish Salad with Cinnamon Dressing

Dark tableware enhances the rich colors of duck with mango chutney, rice with pecans, and orange and radish salad.

ost supermarkets sell frozen whole ducks, but because duck is increasingly in demand, you can sometimes find fresh or frozen breasts, which are needed for the duck salad. Roasted duck skin, or cracklings, is the garnish.

Water chestnuts, also an ingredient in the salad, are not nuts at all but tubers of an aquatic plant. Whole or sliced canned water chestnuts are sold in the Oriental food section of most supermarkets. Occasionally, fresh water chestnuts are available at Chinese groceries. If you use fresh, boil them whole for 15 minutes, cool slightly, then peel and use them as directed in the recipe.

WHAT TO DRINK

Serve a Gewürztraminer or a dry Alsatian Riesling with this menu. If you prefer a touch of sweetness, select a German Riesling from the Rhine area.

SHOPPING LIST AND STAPLES

2 whole boneless duck breasts with skin (about
    1½ pounds total weight)
1 bunch radishes
1 bunch watercress
Small bunch scallions
Small bunch fresh mint, or 2 teaspoons dried
Small bunch fresh parsley (if not using fresh mint)
1 lemon
1 juice orange
4 navel oranges
2 cups chicken stock, preferably homemade (see
    page 9), or canned
8-ounce can sliced water chestnuts
1 stick unsalted butter
¼ cup olive oil
¼ cup mayonnaise, preferably homemade (see
    page 12)
8-ounce jar mango chutney
4 sesame pita breads
1 cup long-grain rice
4-ounce can pecan pieces
2 teaspoons sugar, approximately (optional)
2 teaspoons ground cinnamon
Salt
Freshly ground pepper

UTENSILS

12 x 9-inch roasting pan with rack
Baking sheet
Medium-size heavy-gauge saucepan with cover
Large bowl
2 medium-size bowls, 1 heatproof
Small bowl
Salad spinner (optional)
Measuring cups and spoons
Chef's knife or cleaver
Paring knife
Wooden spoon
Zester or grater
Juicer
Kitchen scissors

START-TO-FINISH STEPS

1. Wash fresh mint or parsley, and dry with paper towels. Reserve 4 mint or parsley sprigs for orange and radish salad recipe, and mince enough mint to measure ¼ cup for rice recipe.
2. Follow duck salad recipe steps 1 through 3.
3. Follow rice recipe steps 1 through 3.
4. Follow duck salad recipe step 4.
5. While duck is roasting, follow rice recipe steps 4 through 6.
6. Follow orange and radish salad recipe steps 1 through 5.
7. Follow duck salad recipe steps 5 through 15 and serve with rice and orange and radish salad.

RECIPES

Warm Duck Salad with Mango Chutney

2 whole boneless duck breasts with skin (about
    1½ pounds total weight)
Salt and freshly ground pepper
8-ounce can sliced water chestnuts
Small bunch scallions
½ cup mango chutney
¼ cup mayonnaise
1 bunch watercress
4 sesame pita breads
1 stick unsalted butter

1. Preheat oven to 475 degrees. Place rack in roasting pan.
2. Wash duck breasts under cold running water and dry with paper towels. Using sharp chef's knife or cleaver, halve breasts. Generously season both sides with salt and pepper.
3. Place breasts, skin-side up, on rack and roast 10 minutes.
4. Reduce oven temperature to 425 degrees and roast another 30 minutes.
5. Remove duck from oven and set aside to rest 10 minutes. Reduce oven temperature to 325 degrees.
6. Meanwhile, drain water chestnuts; set aside.
7. Wash scallions and dry with paper towels. Trim off ends and discard. Thinly slice 3 scallions; reserve remaining scallions for another use.
8. When duck is cool enough to handle, remove skin. With paring knife, scrape off any remaining fat from duck and skin pieces. Reserve skin.
9. Cut duck into 1-inch cubes. Place in medium-size heatproof bowl, cover loosely with foil, and keep warm on top of stove.
10. Using kitchen scissors, cut duck skin into 1½-inch pieces and place on roasting rack. Return pan to oven and

roast skin 10 minutes, or until golden brown and crispy.

11. Meanwhile, combine water chestnuts, scallions, chutney, and mayonnaise in large bowl and stir until blended. Add warm duck cubes and stir gently to combine. Cover loosely with foil and keep warm.

12. Wash watercress and dry in a salad spinner or with paper towels. Remove stems and discard. Divide watercress among 4 dinner plates.

13. Using kitchen scissors, cut pita into triangles and butter insides. Arrange triangles in single layer on baking sheet. Line plate with double thickness of paper towels.

14. Transfer crispy duck skin to paper towels to drain. Place pita bread in oven to toast about 5 minutes.

15. Top watercress with equal portions of duck mixture. Sprinkle each serving with cracklings and serve with toasted pita bread.

Rice with Pecans and Mint

2 cups chicken stock
4-ounce can pecan pieces
1 cup long-grain rice
1 juice orange
¼ cup minced fresh mint, or 2 teaspoons dried
1 teaspoon salt
1 teaspoon freshly ground pepper

1. In medium-size heavy-gauge saucepan, bring stock to a boil over high heat.

2. While stock is heating, coarsely chop enough pecans to measure 1 cup; set aside.

3. Add rice to boiling stock and stir. Reduce heat, cover, and simmer gently 12 to 15 minutes, or until rice is tender and liquid has been absorbed.

4. Wash orange and dry with paper towel. Using zester or grater, remove rind, avoiding white pith as much as possible; reserve rind. Squeeze enough juice to measure ¼ cup.

5. In medium-size bowl, combine pecans, orange rind and juice, mint, salt, and pepper, and stir with fork; set aside.

6. Fluff rice with fork. Add rice to mixture in bowl and toss gently to combine; set aside at room temperature until ready to serve.

Orange and Radish Salad with Cinnamon Dressing

4 navel oranges
1 bunch radishes
1 lemon
¼ cup olive oil
2 teaspoons ground cinnamon
1 to 2 teaspoons sugar (optional)
4 sprigs fresh mint or parsley for garnish (optional)

1. Peel oranges, removing as much white pith as possible. Cut each orange crosswise into ¼-inch-thick rounds; set aside.

2. Wash and trim radishes; dry with paper towels. Thinly slice and set aside.

3. Squeeze lemon to measure 2 tablespoons juice.

4. In small bowl, combine oil, lemon juice, cinnamon, and, if desired, sugar to taste, and beat with fork until blended.

5. Arrange orange and radish slices in alternating rows on each of 4 salad plates and top with dressing. Garnish each serving with a mint or parsley sprig, if desired. Cover with plastic wrap and set aside until ready to serve.

ADDED TOUCHES

For a truly Italian dessert, serve peach halves filled with a rich *cannoli* cream similar to the ricotta cheese filling Neapolitans use to fill fried pastry shells. If fresh peaches are not in season, fill pear halves, or mound the cream on top of strawberries or seedless grapes.

Peaches with Cannoli Cream

1 lemon
1 pound ricotta cheese
½ cup confectioners' sugar
1¼ teaspoons vanilla extract
¾ cup semisweet chocolate chips
4 fresh peaches
Sugar cookies (optional)

1. Wash lemon and dry with paper towel. Grate enough rind to measure 1 tablespoon. Squeeze enough juice to measure 2 tablespoons.

2. In food processor or blender, combine ricotta cheese, confectioners' sugar, lemon rind and juice, and vanilla, and process until smooth. Taste for balance of lemon, sugar, and vanilla, and adjust, if necessary.

3. Turn cream into medium-size bowl and stir in chocolate chips. Cover and refrigerate until ready to serve.

4. Wash peaches and dry with paper towels. Halve and pit peaches. Cut very thin slice from curve of each half to prevent peaches from rolling. Fill cavity of each half with cannoli cream.

5. Divide stuffed peaches among 4 dessert plates and serve with sugar cookies, if desired.

This appetizer, delicious eaten plain or with a creamy dip, is made with plantains—large, thick-skinned yellowish green bananas. Look for plantains in supermarkets or in Spanish or Latin American groceries. You can substitute white or sweet potatoes.

Homemade Plantain Chips

4 plantains
4 cups vegetable oil
Salt

1. Peel and thinly slice plantains.

2. Heat vegetable oil in medium-size heavy-gauge saucepan to 375 degrees.

3. Add small batches of plantain slices to oil and fry 2 to 3 minutes, or until golden. Remove with slotted spoon and drain on paper towels. Sprinkle with salt and serve.

Fran Shinagel
and Delores Custer

MENU 1 (Right)
Herring and Shrimp Salad with Curry Sauce
Danish Apple Cake

MENU 2
Creamy Carrot-Orange Soup
BLT in a Bowl

MENU 3
Cucumber and Buttermilk Soup
Caesar Salad with Homemade Croutons
Norwegian Landgang

When Fran Shinagel and Delores Custer collaborate on menu planning, they like to combine elements from many different cuisines. Having recently worked together in Norway and Denmark, however, they have a particular interest in the foods of these countries. Thus, two of their menus feature Scandinavian dishes.

The ample main-course salad of Menu 1, a beautifully composed platter of pickled herring *(matjes)*, shrimp, and vegetables served with curry sauce, is typical of both Norway and Denmark. It is followed by Danish apple cake, or *aeblekage*, a dessert popular in Delores Custer's hometown, Junction City, Oregon, which has a large Scandinavian population.

In Menu 2, the cooks present an American salad—BLT in a bowl—which, as its name suggests, contains several ingredients usually found between two slices of white toast. Crispy bacon, crunchy romaine lettuce, and sweet cherry tomatoes are combined with creamy Jarlsberg cheese and toasted almonds and then tossed with lemon-garlic dressing. Carrot soup begins this year-round meal.

Menu 3 is a simple and internationally influenced lunch or dinner. The cooks offer a Caesar salad (named for Caesar Cardini, who created the prototype at his restaurant in Tiajuana, Mexico, in 1924), along with a typical Norwegian sandwich called a *landgang*, which literally means "gangplank." In Norway, these long, open-faced sandwiches are served on specially cut wooden boards. A refreshing cucumber and buttermilk soup is the first course.

For this traditional Scandinavian meal, select wooden or unpatterned dinner plates to set off the lovely textures and colors of the herring and shrimp and the accompanying slices of egg, cucumber, red onion, mushrooms, and beets. Layer the apple dessert in one large dish or four individual bowls or ramekins.

Herring and Shrimp Salad with Curry Sauce
Danish Apple Cake

Herring in one form or another are eaten at virtually every Scandinavian meal, even breakfast. Pickled herring, available from most supermarkets and specialty food shops, are a particularly delectable salad component. Whatever type of herring you buy, select a variety that is pickled in vinegar and spices, not packed in sour cream. Herring can be refrigerated in a tightly sealed container for up to a week.

WHAT TO DRINK

Ice-cold beer or a crisp well-chilled white wine would make the best accompaniment to this menu. For the wine, choose Verdicchio, Pinot Grigio, or French Muscadet.

SHOPPING LIST AND STAPLES

½ pound fresh medium-size shrimp
4 pickled herring fillets (about ½ pound total weight)
8 large mushrooms (about ½ pound total weight)
Medium-size cucumber
Medium-size red onion
Large tart apple, such as Granny Smith
4 large eggs
½ pint heavy cream
8-ounce container sour cream
4 tablespoons unsalted butter
⅓ cup mayonnaise, preferably homemade (see page 12)
8-ounce can shoestring or sliced beets
35-ounce jar sweetened applesauce
10-ounce jar red currant jelly
1 teaspoon vanilla extract
4 slices dry home-style white bread
¼ cup granulated sugar
4-ounce can slivered almonds
2 teaspoons curry powder
Salt and freshly ground pepper

UTENSILS

Food processor or blender
Large skillet
Medium-size saucepan
Small saucepan with cover
2 medium-size bowls
2 small bowls
Colander
Strainer
Measuring cups and spoons
Chef's knife
Paring knife
Wooden spoon
Electric mixer

START-TO-FINISH STEPS

Thirty minutes ahead: Set out eggs to come to room temperature for salad recipe.

1. Follow salad recipe steps 1 through 6.
2. Follow apple cake recipe steps 1 through 4.
3. Follow salad recipe steps 7 through 15 and serve.
4. Follow apple cake recipe steps 5 through 7 and serve.

RECIPES

Herring and Shrimp Salad with Curry Sauce

Salt
4 large eggs, at room temperature
½ pound fresh medium-size shrimp
⅔ cup sour cream
⅓ cup mayonnaise
2 teaspoons curry powder
Freshly ground pepper
4 pickled herring fillets (about ½ pound total weight)
8-ounce can shoestring or sliced beets
Medium-size cucumber
Large tart apple, such as Granny Smith
Medium-size red onion
8 large mushrooms (about ½ pound total weight)

1. In medium-size saucepan, bring 2 quarts of lightly salted water to a boil over high heat.
2. While water is heating, place eggs in small saucepan, add enough cold water to cover, and bring water just to a boil over medium-high heat. Cover pan, remove from heat, and set aside 12 minutes.
3. Meanwhile, add unpeeled shrimp to boiling water and cook 3 to 4 minutes, or just until shrimp become opaque and begin to curl.
4. For curry sauce, combine sour cream, mayonnaise, curry powder, and salt and pepper to taste in small bowl and stir until well blended. Turn curry sauce into 4 small ramekins or bowls; set aside.
5. Turn shrimp into colander and run under cold water to

cool. To remove shells, lift off two or three shell segments at once and, holding tail, pull shrimp out of shells. Leave tails on. With sharp paring knife, slit down back and lift out black vein. Set shrimp aside.

6. Rinse eggs in colander under cold water and transfer to bowl of ice water; set aside about 10 minutes.

7. Peel eggs and set aside to cool completely.

8. Drain herring fillets, if necessary, and cut crosswise into 1-inch-wide pieces.

9. Turn beets into strainer and rinse under cold running water; set aside to drain.

10. Wash cucumber and dry with paper towels. Using fork, score peel lengthwise; repeat, turning cucumber until entire circumference is scored. Cut cucumber crosswise into thin slices; set aside.

11. Wash and dry apple. Halve, core, and cut apple into ½-inch dice; set aside.

12. Peel onion and cut crosswise into thin slices. Separate slices into individual rings; set aside.

13. Wipe mushrooms with damp paper towel. Cut into thin slices; set aside.

14. When eggs are completely cool, slice with sharp knife.

15. Divide apple, herring, beets, mushrooms, cucumber, eggs, shrimp, and onion among 4 dinner plates, arranging them in an attractive pattern. Serve with curry sauce on the side.

Danish Apple Cake

4 slices dry home-style white bread
4-ounce can slivered almonds
4 tablespoons unsalted butter
¼ cup granulated sugar
35-ounce jar sweetened applesauce
½ cup heavy cream
1 teaspoon vanilla extract
¼ cup red currant jelly

1. Place medium-size bowl and beaters for whipping cream in freezer to chill.

2. Trim crusts from bread. In food processor or blender, process enough bread to measure 1 cup coarse crumbs; transfer to small bowl; set aside.

3. In food processor or blender, coarsely chop almonds; set aside.

4. In large skillet, melt butter over medium-low heat. Add bread crumbs, almonds, and 2 tablespoons sugar, and sauté, stirring constantly, 5 to 7 minutes, or until crumbs are golden brown. Remove pan from heat and set mixture aside to cool.

5. Arranging in alternate layers and beginning and ending with crumbs, divide crumb mixture and applesauce among four 1-cup serving bowls or ramekins. There should be three layers of crumbs and two of applesauce.

6. Combine cream with remaining 2 tablespoons sugar in chilled bowl and beat with electric mixer until combined. Add vanilla to cream and beat just until soft peaks form.

7. Top each serving with 3 separate dollops of whipped cream and garnish each dollop with 1 teaspoon of red

currant jelly. Serve apple cake with remaining whipped cream on the side, if desired.

ADDED TOUCH

Boller are round sweetened rolls often served in Scandinavia; they are easy to make with this food processor method.

Boller

4 tablespoons unsalted butter
½ cup milk
Two ¼-ounce packages dry yeast
1 egg, at room temperature
2¾ to 3 cups all-purpose flour
¼ cup granulated sugar
½ teaspoon salt
½ teaspoon cardamom
Vegetable shortening for greasing bowl and cookie sheet

1. Combine butter and milk in small saucepan and heat over low heat until mixture is warm to the touch.

2. Meanwhile, combine yeast and ¼ cup warm, *not* hot, tap water in 1-cup measure and stir until yeast is dissolved; set aside.

3. In large skillet, bring 5 cups of water to a boil.

4. For glaze, crack egg into small bowl and beat until blended. Transfer 1 tablespoon egg to a cup and beat with 1 tablespoon water; set aside. Reserve remaining egg.

5. Combine 2¾ cups flour, sugar, salt, and cardamom in food processor fitted with steel blade and process about 20 seconds.

6. With machine running, add yeast mixture, butter and milk, and remaining beaten egg through feed tube, and process until dough gathers around blade. Dough should be soft and somewhat sticky. If too dry, add warm water by teaspoonfuls and process just until proper consistency is obtained; if too moist, add remaining ¼ cup flour, 1 tablespoon at a time, and process until proper consistency is obtained.

7. Grease large mixing bowl and medium-size baking sheet.

8. Scrape dough into prepared bowl, cover with damp towel or plastic wrap, and place on upper rack in cold oven. Place skillet of boiling water on lower rack under bowl, close oven door, and let dough rise about 45 minutes, or until doubled in bulk.

9. Remove bowl from oven and punch down dough. Knead several times in bowl. Pinch off 10 to 12 pieces of dough, and form into balls about the size of golf balls. Place balls several inches apart on prepared baking sheet, cover with damp towel or plastic wrap, and set aside about 20 minutes.

10. Remove skillet of water from oven and preheat oven to 375 degrees.

11. Brush tops of balls with egg glaze and bake 15 to 20 minutes, or until golden brown.

12. Transfer rolls to wire rack to cool.

Creamy Carrot-Orange Soup
BLT in a Bowl

The carrot soup has a refreshing—and surprising—flavor from the addition of orange juice and zest. For the smoothest texture, purée the soup in a blender or food processor in small amounts. For a lighter variation, omit the heavy cream; the soup will still be very good. You can easily double this recipe and freeze the soup for future meals.

All of the ingredients for the salad can be purchased year round. Most of the year, tomatoes look good but taste like damp cardboard; be sure to use sweet cherry tomatoes except in the summer, when vine-ripened tomatoes are available.

This casual soup and salad meal features a fragrant carrot and orange soup and a BLT salad as the main course. Warm bread and mugs of ale or beer are the perfect complements.

WHAT TO DRINK

Cold ale, especially a malty English or Belgian import, would complement this menu nicely. If you prefer wine, try a simple Soave or a white Mâcon or Saint-Véran.

SHOPPING LIST AND STAPLES

½ pound sliced bacon
Small head romaine lettuce
Small head iceberg lettuce
1 pint cherry tomatoes
½ pound carrots
Large onion
1 large plus 1 small clove garlic
Small bunch parsley

Medium-size lemon
1 orange
½ pint heavy cream
3 tablespoons unsalted butter
½ pound Jarlsberg cheese
¼ pound Parmesan cheese
4 cups chicken stock, preferably homemade
    (see page 9), or canned
¾ cup vegetable oil
1 loaf Italian bread
4-ounce can slivered almonds
2 tablespoons long-grain rice
¼ teaspoon sugar
Salt and freshly ground pepper

UTENSILS

Blender or food processor
Medium-size skillet
Medium-size heavy-gauge saucepan with cover
Baking sheet
2 small bowls
Salad spinner (optional)
Measuring cups and spoons
Chef's knife
Serrated bread knife (optional)
Paring knife

2 wooden spoons
Slotted spatula
Whisk
Juicer
Grater (if not using food processor)
Zester

START-TO-FINISH STEPS

1. Follow soup recipe steps 1 through 5.
2. While soup is simmering, follow salad recipe steps 1 through 8.
3. Follow soup recipe step 6.
4. Follow salad recipe steps 9 through 11.
5. Follow soup recipe steps 7 and 8.
6. While soup is reheating, follow salad recipe step 12.
7. Follow soup recipe step 9 and serve as first course.
8. Follow salad recipe steps 13 and 14, and serve.

RECIPES

Creamy Carrot-Orange Soup

Large onion
½ pound carrots
Small clove garlic
3 tablespoons unsalted butter
2 tablespoons long-grain rice

8 parsley sprigs
1 orange
4 cups chicken stock
¼ teaspoon sugar
½ cup heavy cream

1. Peel and coarsely chop enough onion to measure 1 cup. Peel, trim, and cut enough carrots crosswise into ¼-inch-thick slices to measure 1½ cups. Crush garlic under flat blade of chef's knife; remove peel and discard.
2. In medium-size heavy-gauge saucepan, melt butter over low heat. Add onion, carrots, garlic, and rice, and sauté over medium heat, stirring occasionally, about 5 minutes, or until vegetables become fragrant.
3. Wash parsley and dry with paper towels.
4. Rinse and dry orange; halve crosswise. Using zester or paring knife, remove rind from one half and then squeeze juice of that half into small bowl; set rind and juice aside. Cut four ¼-inch-thick slices from remaining half and reserve for garnish.
5. Add stock, orange rind, 4 parsley sprigs, and sugar to vegetables, and bring to a boil. Reduce heat and simmer gently, covered, 25 to 30 minutes, or until vegetables are tender.
6. Remove parsley sprigs from soup and discard; set soup aside to cool slightly.
7. Transfer soup to blender and purée; or purée in batches in food processor.
8. Return soup to pan, stir in orange juice and cream, and reheat briefly over medium-low heat; do *not* boil.
9. Divide soup among individual bowls and garnish each serving with an orange slice topped with a parsley sprig.

BLT in a Bowl

Small head romaine lettuce
Small head iceberg lettuce
½ cup slivered almonds
½ pound sliced bacon
1 pint cherry tomatoes
½ pound Jarlsberg cheese
¼ pound Parmesan cheese
Medium-size lemon
Large clove garlic
¾ cup vegetable oil
1 loaf Italian bread
Salt
Freshly ground pepper

1. Preheat oven to 300 degrees.
2. Wash heads of lettuce and dry in salad spinner or with paper towels. Remove and discard any bruised or discolored leaves. If desired, remove and discard tough ribs from large romaine leaves. Refrigerate lettuce until ready to serve.
3. Arrange almonds in single layer on baking sheet and toast, shaking pan occasionally, 12 to 15 minutes, or until golden.
4. Meanwhile, cut bacon slices crosswise into 1-inch-wide

pieces. Line a plate with double thickness of paper towels. In medium-size skillet, fry bacon over medium-high heat, stirring occasionally, 6 to 8 minutes, or until crisp.
5. While bacon is frying, wash cherry tomatoes and dry with paper towels. Remove stems, if necessary, and halve tomatoes; set aside.
6. With slotted spatula, transfer bacon to paper towels to drain.
7. Remove almonds from oven and set aside to cool.
8. Using food processor fitted with shredding disk or on coarse side of grater, shred Jarlsberg; set aside. In processor fitted with steel blade or with grater, finely grate enough Parmesan to measure ½ cup; set aside.
9. Squeeze enough lemon juice to measure 3 tablespoons.
10. Crush garlic under flat blade of chef's knife; remove peel and discard.
11. Combine lemon juice and garlic in small bowl. Beating with whisk, add oil in a slow, steady stream and beat until well blended. Set aside until ready to serve.
12. Remove lettuce from refrigerator. Gather leaves into stacks and cut crosswise into ½-inch-wide shreds. Place lettuce in large salad bowl. Add bacon, tomatoes, cheeses, and toasted almonds, and toss to combine.
13. Cut bread crosswise into 1-inch-thick slices and place in napkin-lined bowl or basket.
14. Beat dressing to recombine; remove garlic and discard. Add dressing to salad and toss until evenly coated. Add salt and freshly ground pepper to taste, and serve salad with bread.

ADDED TOUCH

The juice of cranberries combines with fresh orange juice and orange-flavored liqueur in this tangy dessert sorbet, which must be prepared well in advance of serving time.

Cranberry Sorbet

12-ounce can frozen cranberry juice
    concentrate
1½ cups freshly squeezed orange juice
¼ cup Triple Sec or other orange-flavored
    liqueur

1. Combine all ingredients with 1¼ cups cold water in container of blender or food processor and process until combined.
2. Pour mixture into 2 metal ice-cube trays without the sections or into 9-inch-round metal cake pan, cover with foil, and place in freezer for about 2½ hours, or until firm but not solid.
3. Spoon frozen mixture into medium-size bowl and break up any firm pieces with wooden spoon.
4. With electric mixer, whip sorbet until smooth and pack into quart-size container with tight-fitting lid. Return to freezer for at least 1 to 1½ hours before serving.
5. Remove sorbet from freezer and divide among 4 bowls or goblets. If frozen solid, place in refrigerator 15 to 20 minutes to soften slightly before serving.

Cucumber and Buttermilk Soup
Caesar Salad with Homemade Croutons
Norwegian Landgang

A Caesar salad and an open-faced Norwegian landgang *are a filling follow-up to the tangy cucumber and buttermilk soup.*

The *landgang* is actually many sandwiches in one. The cooks suggest using at least five toppings, but you can use whatever you have on hand. When assembling the *landgang*, be sure to spread the cut surfaces of the bread with a thick coating of unsalted butter (or perhaps herbed butter, cream cheese, or sweet, dill-flavored mustard) to help anchor the toppings securely and to prevent any juices from penetrating the bread.

WHAT TO DRINK

A cold white wine with considerable body would be a good match for these dishes. A white Burgundy—Chablis is an excellent choice or California Chardonnay—is ideal.

SHOPPING LIST AND STAPLES

¼ pound thinly sliced smoked salmon
¼ pound sliced cooked ham
4 medium-size cucumbers (about 2½ pounds total weight)
2 large heads romaine lettuce
Small head leaf or Bibb lettuce
1 bunch watercress for garnish (optional)
1 pint cherry tomatoes
Small red bell pepper for garnish (optional)
3 to 4 shallots, or small onion
2 large cloves garlic
Small bunch fresh dill for garnish (optional)
2 large lemons
4-ounce can liver pâté, or ¼ pound sliced good-quality liverwurst
1 egg
1½ cups buttermilk
7 tablespoons unsalted butter, approximately
¼ pound Parmesan cheese
¼ pound Jarlsberg cheese, thinly sliced
¼ pound Nøkkelost cheese, thickly sliced
½ cup chicken stock, preferably homemade (see page 9), or canned
¾ cup olive oil, approximately
8-ounce jar baby dill gherkins
2-ounce tin anchovy fillets (optional)
2 teaspoons Worcestershire sauce
1 long unsliced loaf firm bread, such as French or Italian

81

4 slices dry home-style white bread
Salt and freshly ground black and white pepper

UTENSILS

Blender or food processor
Medium-size skillet or sauté pan
2 medium-size saucepans, 1 nonaluminum
Baking sheet
Platter
Small bowl
Colander
Measuring cups and spoons
Chef's knife
Paring knife
2 wooden spoons
Slotted metal spatula
Rubber spatula
Vegetable peeler
Juicer
Grater (if not using food processor)

START-TO-FINISH STEPS

1. Wash and dry greens for sandwich and salad recipes; refrigerate until ready to serve. If using watercress, wash, trim off stems, and discard; refrigerate. Rinse and dry dill. Snip enough dill to measure 1 tablespoon, if using, for soup recipe. Set aside a few sprigs for garnish for sandwich recipe; reserve remainder for another use. Crush garlic for salad and croutons recipes; remove peels and discard. Wash and dry 1 cucumber. Using fork, score peel lengthwise; repeat, turning cucumber until entirely scored. Cut cucumber crosswise into thin slices; reserve 8 slices for soup recipe and remainder for sandwich recipe.
2. Follow soup recipe steps 1 through 3.
3. While vegetables are sautéing, follow salad recipe steps 1 through 3 and croutons recipe step 1.
4. Follow soup recipe steps 4 and 5.
5. Follow croutons recipe steps 2 and 3, and sandwich recipe steps 1 through 5.
6. Follow croutons recipe steps 4 through 7.
7. Follow salad recipe steps 4 and 5, and sandwich recipe steps 6 and 7.
8. Follow soup recipe steps 6 and 7, and serve as first course.
9. Follow salad recipe step 6 and serve with sandwich.

RECIPES

Cucumber and Buttermilk Soup

3 medium-size cucumbers, plus 8 slices for garnish
3 to 4 shallots, or small onion
3 tablespoons unsalted butter
½ cup chicken stock
1½ cups buttermilk
Salt and freshly ground white pepper
1 tablespoon snipped fresh dill (optional)

1. Peel cucumbers and halve lengthwise. Using teaspoon, scoop out seeds and discard. Cut each half into ½-inch-thick slices; set aside. You should have about 3 cups.
2. Peel and coarsely chop enough shallots or onion to measure 3 tablespoons.
3. In medium-size nonaluminum saucepan, melt butter over low heat. Add cucumbers and shallots or onion, raise heat to medium-low, and sauté, stirring occasionally, 8 to 10 minutes, or until vegetables are softened but not brown.
4. Transfer vegetables to blender or, in batches, to food processor. Add stock and process about 1 minute, or until fairly smooth and thick.
5. If serving soup chilled, add buttermilk and salt and pepper to taste, and process about 10 seconds, or just until blended. Cover container and refrigerate until ready to serve. If serving hot, return purée to saucepan; set aside.
6. Just before serving, for chilled soup, process briefly to recombine. For hot soup, bring to a simmer over medium heat. Stir in buttermilk and salt and pepper to taste, reduce heat to medium-low, and stir constantly until hot; do *not* boil. If the soup gets too hot and appears curdled, return to blender and process until smooth. Taste soup and adjust seasoning.
7. Divide soup among 4 bowls and garnish each serving with 2 cucumber slices. Sprinkle with dill, if desired, and serve.

Caesar Salad with Homemade Croutons

¼ pound Parmesan cheese
Large lemon
Large clove garlic, crushed and peeled
1 egg
2 teaspoons Worcestershire sauce
Salt and freshly ground black pepper
½ cup olive oil
2-ounce tin anchovy fillets (optional)
2 large heads romaine lettuce
Homemade Croutons (see following recipe)

1. Using grater or food processor fitted with steel blade, grate enough Parmesan to measure 1 cup. Turn into small bowl and set aside.
2. Squeeze enough lemon juice to measure ¼ cup.
3. For dressing, combine garlic, lemon juice, egg, Worcestershire sauce, and salt and pepper to taste in food processor or blender and process 6 to 8 seconds, or until well blended. With machine running, add oil in a slow, steady stream and process until thick and creamy.
4. Drain anchovies, if using, and coarsely chop enough to measure 1 tablespoon; set aside.
5. Tear romaine into bite-size pieces; small inner leaves can be left whole. Place in large salad bowl and refrigerate until ready to serve.
6. Add cheese to salad and top with croutons and anchovies. Pour dressing over salad and toss gently to combine. Add more salt and pepper, if desired.

Homemade Croutons

4 slices dry home-style white bread
3 tablespoons olive oil
Large clove garlic, crushed and peeled

1. Preheat oven to 300 degrees.
2. If desired, trim crusts from bread. Cut enough bread into ½-inch cubes to measure 2 cups.
3. Arrange bread cubes in single layer on baking sheet and toast about 15 minutes, or until crisp.
4. Remove toasted cubes from oven and set aside.
5. Line a platter with paper towels.
6. In medium-size skillet or sauté pan, heat oil over medium heat. Add garlic and bread cubes, and sauté over medium-high heat, stirring and shaking skillet, 5 to 7 minutes, or until cubes are golden.
7. With slotted metal spatula, transfer croutons to paper-towel-lined platter to drain.

Norwegian Landgang

4-ounce can liver pâté, or ¼ pound sliced good-quality liverwurst
1 pint cherry tomatoes
Small red bell pepper for garnish (optional)
Large lemon
8-ounce jar baby dill gherkins
1 long unsliced loaf firm bread, such as French or Italian
4 tablespoons unsalted butter, approximately
¼ pound thinly sliced smoked salmon
¼ pound sliced cooked ham
¼ pound Jarlsberg cheese, thinly sliced
¼ pound Nøkkelost cheese, thickly sliced
½ cucumber, scored and cut into thin slices
Small head leaf or Bibb lettuce
Fresh dill sprigs for garnish (optional)
1 bunch watercress for garnish (optional)

1. If using pâté, cut into ½-inch-thick slices; set aside.
2. Wash cherry tomatoes and dry with paper towels. Remove stems from 4 tomatoes, if necessary, and cut tomatoes in half. Reserve remainder for another use.
3. Wash red bell pepper, if using, and dry with paper towel. Halve, core, and seed pepper. Cut one half lengthwise into ¼-inch strips. Reserve remaining half for another use.
4. Wash lemon and dry with paper towel. Halve lemon crosswise; cut one half into wedges and cut remaining half into thin slices; set aside.
5. Drain as many gherkins as desired.
6. Trim bottom crust of long loaf, if necessary, to sit flat on serving board or platter. Halve loaf lengthwise and generously butter cut side of each half. Place bread on long wooden cutting board or other flat serving platter.
7. Assemble pâté, salmon, ham, cheeses, cucumber, tomatoes, lemon, lettuce, and gherkins. Arrange ingredients attractively on top of bread halves. Garnish platter with dill sprigs, watercress, and pepper strips, if using, and set aside until ready to serve.

Italian prune plums, the primary component of this cake-like dessert, are available for a short time in late summer.

Plum Crisp

2 pounds fresh Italian prune plums, or 2 pints blueberries
2 to 4 tablespoons firmly packed Turbinado or other light brown sugar
1 tablespoon all-purpose flour
Pinch of mace
Pinch of cinnamon

Topping:
1 cup granulated sugar
1 cup all-purpose flour
1 teaspoon baking powder
¼ teaspoon salt (optional)
1 stick unsalted butter, softened and cut into small pieces
1 egg, at room temperature

Garnish (optional):
½ pint heavy cream or crème fraîche, or 1 pint vanilla ice cream

1. If using whipped cream for garnish, place medium-size bowl and beaters in freezer to chill.
2. Preheat oven to 350 degrees. Set rack in center.
3. Wash and dry plums or blueberries. Halve and pit plums. Remove and discard any bad berries.
4. In large bowl, combine 2 tablespoons light brown sugar, flour, mace, and cinnamon. Add plums or blueberries, and stir to coat evenly. Taste and add more sugar, if desired.
5. Turn mixture into 10-inch quiche dish, cast-iron skillet, or other ovenproof dish at least 1½ inches deep. (Do not use a springform pan or the juice will bubble out.)
6. Prepare topping: In food processor fitted with steel blade, combine sugar, flour, baking powder, and salt, and process 10 to 15 seconds. Or, combine dry ingredients in large mixing bowl.
7. If using processor, add butter and process 10 to 15 seconds, or until mixture is crumbly. Or, cut in butter with pastry blender or two knives.
8. Add egg and process about 10 seconds, or until dough starts to gather on blades. Or, stir and toss with fork. Batter will resemble cookie dough.
9. Spoon dough over plum mixture. Using long, thin knife or icing spatula, spread batter over fruit as evenly as possible. Some fruit may not be covered completely.
10. Place a sheet of foil on oven rack to catch any drippings and place dish or skillet in center of oven. Bake 1 hour to 1 hour and 15 minutes, or until top is golden brown.
11. If using whipped cream for garnish, just before serving place heavy cream in chilled bowl and beat with electric mixer until soft peaks form.
12. Remove plum crisp from oven and set aside to cool.
13. Divide plum crisp among dessert bowls and top each serving with a dollop of whipped cream or crème fraîche, or a scoop of ice cream, if desired.

Deborah Madison

Fresh vegetables of all types play an important role in Deborah Madison's cooking. Although she is not a strict vegetarian, she likes to create new recipes without meat, featuring such products as tofu. She also strives to streamline the multistep methods and long preparation times often associated with vegetarian meals.

Menu 1 is a soup and salad meal that can be made year round, although this cook prefers to serve it in the autumn, when the crisp weather piques appetites. To save time, she purées the soup in a blender after it has simmered briefly, and offers the option of using precooked *cannellini* beans, which do not require soaking, in the salad.

An easy indoor or outdoor picnic, Menu 2 gives guests a chance to create their own salads from a variety of fresh vegetables—green beans, new potatoes, red bell peppers, and tomatoes among them. Hard-boiled eggs, goat cheese, and French bread are the accompaniments.

The highly textured salad of Menu 3 is a mixture of tofu, celery, red or green bell peppers, and carrots that can be served on greens or between slices of whole-wheat bread. Because the first-course sugar snap pea soup cooks for just five minutes, it retains its bright color and fresh pea flavor.

For a substantial family or company meal, serve red bell pepper soup followed by a white bean salad mounded on shredded romaine and radicchio. If you like, offer a basket of assorted warm rolls on the side.

Red Bell Pepper Soup
White Bean Salad with
Romaine and Radicchio

This meal begins with a flavorful red bell pepper soup to which *crème fraîche* may be added. *Crème fraîche* is a French cultivated cream product with a silky texture that resembles sour cream. It is costly and not often available commercially, but you can make your own reasonable facsimile. Bring a half pint of heavy cream and a half pint of sour cream to room temperature, then whisk together. Pour the mixture into a clean glass jar, cover tightly, let stand at room temperature for 6 to 8 hours, and then refrigerate. It will keep for 10 days.

White *cannellini*, a variety of kidney beans, are the basis for the main-course salad. These imported beans are available dried or precooked in cans. While the cook prefers dried beans, you can use the canned variety with success. If you do, start with step 5 of the recipe.

WHAT TO DRINK

A red wine would complement the flavors in this menu. Your choices range from a light-bodied French Beaujolais or California Gamay Beaujolais to a more robust wine such as a Zinfandel or a Chianti Classico.

SHOPPING LIST AND STAPLES

2 large red bell peppers (about 1 pound total weight)
4 small ripe tomatoes (about 1 pound total weight)
1 head romaine lettuce
Small head radicchio
Small fennel bulb (about 10 ounces) with feathery tops, or small bunch celery with leaves
Large yellow onion (about ¾ pound)
Small red onion
1 clove garlic
Selection of fresh herbs, such as parsley, chervil, thyme, or tarragon
1 lemon
4 cups chicken stock, preferably homemade (see page 9), or canned (optional)
8-ounce container crème fraîche
¼ pound hard grating cheese, such as pecorino Romano, Asiago, or Parmesan
½ cup plus 2 tablespoons olive oil, preferably extra-virgin
¼ cup white or red wine vinegar or sherry vinegar
7-ounce jar Niçoise or Kalamata olives
1¾ cups dried cannellini, Great Northern, or Navy beans, or two 19-ounce cans

½ teaspoon each dried rosemary, thyme, savory, and oregano or marjoram
1 bay leaf
Salt and freshly ground black pepper

UTENSILS

Blender or food processor
Large heavy-gauge saucepan
Medium-size heavy-gauge saucepan
Kettle
2 large bowls, 1 heatproof
2 medium-size bowls
Small bowl
Colander
Large strainer
Measuring cups and spoons
Chef's knife
Paring knife
2 wooden spoons
Rubber spatula
Small whisk
Grater (if not using processor)

START-TO-FINISH STEPS

The night before or about two and a half hours ahead: If using dried beans, follow bean salad recipe steps 1 through 4.

1. Follow soup recipe steps 1 through 6.
2. Follow bean salad recipe steps 5 through 9.
3. Follow soup recipe step 7.
4. Follow bean salad recipe steps 10 through 13.
5. Follow soup recipe step 8 and bean salad recipe step 14.
6. Follow soup recipe steps 9 through 13 and serve as first course.
7. Follow bean salad recipe steps 15 and 16, and serve.

RECIPES

Red Bell Pepper Soup

Large yellow onion (about ¾ pound)
2 tablespoons olive oil, preferably extra-virgin
2 large red bell peppers (about 1 pound total weight)
1 bay leaf
1 sprig parsley

½ teaspoon each dried rosemary, thyme, savory, and
    oregano or marjoram
Salt
4 small ripe tomatoes (about 1 pound total weight)
1 clove garlic
4 cups cooking liquid from dried beans, if using, or
    chicken stock, water, or any combination
1 lemon
Freshly ground black pepper
8-ounce container crème fraîche

1. Peel and cut onion into ¼-inch-thick slices.
2. In medium-size heavy-gauge saucepan, heat oil over
low heat. Add onion to pan and stir until slices are coated
with oil. Raise heat to medium and sauté onions, stirring
occasionally, 2 to 3 minutes, or until softened.
3. Meanwhile, wash and dry peppers. Halve, core, and
seed peppers; cut lengthwise into ¼-inch-wide strips.
4. Add pepper strips, bay leaf, parsley, dried herbs, and 1
teaspoon salt to pan, and sauté, stirring occasionally, 2 to 3
minutes, or until peppers are soft.
5. Meanwhile, wash tomatoes and dry with paper towels.
Core and coarsely chop tomatoes. Peel and chop garlic.
6. Add tomatoes and garlic to pan, cover, and stir 15
minutes.
7. Remove bay leaf. Add 4 cups liquid to pan and bring to a
boil. Reduce heat and simmer gently 15 minutes.
8. Remove pan from heat and set soup aside to cool. Halve
lemon, squeeze juice from one half, and reserve remaining
half for another use; set juice aside.
9. Transfer mixture to blender and purée. Or, in batches,
purée mixture in food processor.
10. Pour purée through strainer set over medium-size
bowl, pressing solids left in strainer with back of spoon to
extrude as much liquid as possible; discard solids.
11. Return soup to pan. Add salt, pepper, and lemon juice
to taste, and set pan over medium heat 2 to 3 minutes, or
until soup is heated through.
12. Turn crème fraîche into small serving bowl.
13. Pour soup into tureen and serve with crème fraîche on
the side.

White Bean Salad with Romaine
and Radicchio

1¾ cups dried cannellini, Great Northern, or Navy
    beans, or two 19-ounce cans
Salt
¼ cup white or red wine vinegar or sherry vinegar
½ cup olive oil, preferably extra-virgin
Small fennel bulb (about 10 ounces) with feathery tops, or
    2 stalks celery with leaves
Small red onion
Selection of fresh herbs, such as parsley, chervil, thyme,
    or tarragon
¼ pound hard grating cheese, such as pecorino Romano,
    Asiago, or Parmesan
7-ounce jar Niçoise or Kalamata olives
1 head romaine lettuce

Small head radicchio
Freshly ground black pepper

1. If using dried beans, bring 10 cups of water to a boil in
kettle over high heat.
2. Meanwhile, place beans in large strainer or colander
and rinse under cold water. Remove any foreign matter.
3. Turn beans into large heatproof bowl. Pour boiling
water over beans and set aside to soak 1 hour.
4. Transfer beans to large heavy-gauge saucepan, add 1
teaspoon salt, and bring to a boil over high heat. Reduce
heat and simmer gently, checking occasionally to see if
water needs replenishing, 1 to 1½ hours, or until beans are
tender but not mushy. Rinse and dry bowl.
5. Turn cooked beans into colander set over large bowl;
reserve bean liquid, if desired, for red pepper soup recipe.
Turn drained beans into medium-size bowl and set aside to
cool slightly, if using same day. If preparing the night
before, refrigerate beans overnight, then bring to room
temperature before using. If using canned beans, turn
into colander and rinse under cold running water; drain.
Turn beans into medium-size bowl; set aside.
6. For dressing, combine 2 tablespoons vinegar and ½
teaspoon salt in small bowl. Whisking vigorously, add olive
oil in a slow, steady stream and continue whisking until
blended. Taste and add more vinegar, if desired.
7. Pour half the dressing over the beans and stir gently to
combine; reserve remaining dressing.
8. Reserve fennel tops for garnish. Remove tough outer
layer from fennel bulb and quarter bulb. Cut out core and
discard. Cut bulb quarters crosswise into ¼-inch-thick
slices. Cut slices into 1-inch-long pieces; add to beans.
9. Peel and halve red onion; cut crosswise into ⅛-inch-
thick slices, then into ¼-inch-wide pieces; add to beans.
10. Wash herbs and dry with paper towels. Remove stems
and discard. Coarsely chop enough herbs to measure 5
tablespoons. Add 3½ tablespoons herbs to beans and reserve remainder for garnish.
11. Using food processor or grater, grate enough cheese to
measure 1 cup. Add grated cheese to beans.
12. Drain 12 olives. Remove and discard pits. Coarsely
chop olives and add to beans.
13. Gently combine salad ingredients. Adjust seasoning
by adding more salt or vinegar; set aside.
14. Remove large outer leaves from romaine. Wash tender
inner romaine leaves and dry with paper towels. Rinse and
dry radicchio; separate leaves. Stack romaine leaves and
cut crosswise into ¼-inch-wide strips. Stack radicchio
leaves and cut crosswise into fine shreds. You will need
about 6 cups of mixed greens. Combine greens in large
bowl, cover, and refrigerate.
15. Add reserved dressing to greens and toss until evenly
coated. Line serving dish with greens.
16. Add freshly ground pepper to beans and stir gently to
combine. Taste and adjust seasonings, if necessary. Spoon
bean mixture into center of dish, leaving generous border
of greens. Garnish bean mixture with remaining herbs
and feathery fennel tops, and serve.

Summer Vegetable Salad with Herb Mayonnaise
Goat Cheese with Rosemary,
Black Pepper, and Olive Oil

A picnic can be as successful indoors as out with a good wine, a selection of finger foods, and—maybe—a blanket on the floor.

The elements of this colorful meal can be varied according to your own taste and to the vegetables that are at their peak in the garden or market. In the spring and summer months, try cucumbers, sweet onions, asparagus, and artichokes. For a winter picnic indoors, serve broccoli, cauliflower, fennel, and red or golden beets.

If you can get a good eating Parmesan, such as a relatively young Parmigiano-Reggiano, serve it with the goat cheese. Both are delicious with slices of French bread.

The herb mayonnaise is whisked by hand in this recipe, but you can easily make it in a blender or food processor to save time. See page 12 for instructions.

WHAT TO DRINK

The cook prefers a Beaujolais or a chilled rosé here, but a young Chianti or Zinfandel would be equally satisfying.

SHOPPING LIST AND STAPLES

¾ pound small new potatoes
¾ pound green beans
2 medium-size red bell peppers (about ½ pound total weight)
2 medium-size ripe tomatoes (about 1 pound total weight)
Small bunch fresh rosemary, or 1 to 2 teaspoons dried
Small bunch fresh thyme (optional)
Selection of other fresh herbs, such as parsley, chives, chervil, tarragon, or marjoram
Medium-size clove garlic
1 lemon, or 1 tablespoon tarragon vinegar
3 eggs
12-ounce log goat cheese, such as Montrachet (without ash), or round chèvre
⅔ cup olive, peanut, or vegetable oil
6 tablespoons extra-virgin olive oil, approximately
1 teaspoon balsamic or sherry vinegar
2-ounce tin anchovy fillets, packed in oil
7-ounce jar small black olives, such as Niçoise or Gaeta
Salt
Freshly ground black pepper

UTENSILS

Large sauté pan
Medium-size saucepan
Small saucepan with cover
Baking dish
Medium-size bowl
Colander
Measuring cups and spoons
Chef's knife
Serrated bread knife
Paring knife
Wooden spoon
Small whisk
Metal tongs (optional)

START-TO-FINISH STEPS

Thirty minutes ahead: Set out eggs to come to room temperature for salad recipe.

1. Follow vegetable salad recipe step 1.
2. Follow goat cheese recipe steps 1 through 4.
3. Follow vegetable salad recipe steps 2 through 13.
4. Follow herb mayonnaise recipe steps 1 through 7.
5. Follow vegetable salad recipe steps 14 through 16, goat cheese recipe step 5, and serve.

RECIPES

Summer Vegetable Salad with Herb Mayonnaise

¾ pound small new potatoes
¼ cup extra-virgin olive oil, approximately
Salt and freshly ground black pepper
Small bunch fresh thyme (optional)
2 eggs, at room temperature
¾ pound green beans
2 medium-size red bell peppers (about ½ pound total weight)
2-ounce tin anchovy fillets, packed in oil
7-ounce jar small black olives, such as Niçoise or Gaeta
1 teaspoon balsamic or sherry vinegar
2 medium-size ripe tomatoes (about 1 pound total weight)
Herb Mayonnaise (see following recipe)

1. Preheat oven to 425 degrees.
2. Wash potatoes under cold running water and dry with paper towels. Place potatoes in baking dish. Drizzle with 1 tablespoon olive oil, and turn potatoes to coat evenly. Sprinkle with salt and pepper. Add 2 to 3 sprigs fresh thyme, if using, and ¼ cup water to dish. Cover with foil and roast potatoes 15 to 20 minutes, or until they can be pierced easily with tip of knife.
3. Meanwhile, place eggs in small saucepan, add enough cold water to cover, and bring to a boil over high heat.
4. While eggs are coming to a boil, bring 2 quarts of water for beans to a boil in medium-size saucepan over high heat.
5. When eggs have come to a boil, turn off heat, cover pan, and set aside 6 minutes.
6. Meanwhile, place beans in colander and rinse under cold running water. Trim off ends and discard. Break any extra-long beans in two so that they are no longer than 3½ to 4 inches.
7. Add beans to boiling water. Return water to a boil and cook beans 5 to 8 minutes, or until crisp-tender.
8. Meanwhile, turn eggs into colander and run under cold water to cool. Set eggs aside.
9. Wash peppers and dry with paper towels. Halve, core, and seed peppers. Cut lengthwise into ¼-inch-wide strips (see illustration on following page). If strips are very long, cut in half. Set aside.
10. Turn green beans into colander and refresh under cold running water. Set aside to drain.

11. Heat 1½ tablespoons olive oil in large sauté pan over high heat. When oil is hot, add pepper strips and sauté, shaking pan to coat them evenly. When peppers are warm to the touch, add about ¼ cup water to pan, reduce heat to medium, and cook another 2 to 3 minutes, or until peppers begin to soften and water has cooked away.

12. While peppers are cooking, test potatoes and, if done, remove from oven; set aside. Drain anchovies and blot dry with paper towel. Slice anchovies lengthwise into thin strips and set aside. Drain olives.

13. Raise heat under peppers to high, sprinkle with vinegar, and season with salt and pepper to taste. Remove pan from heat; set aside.

14. Wash tomatoes and dry with paper towels. Core and halve tomatoes; cut each half into thirds.

15. Peel eggs and quarter lengthwise. Halve potatoes.

16. Divide beans, peppers, tomatoes, potatoes, and eggs among 4 plates. Top eggs with olive oil and anchovies. Sprinkle potatoes with coarsely ground black pepper to taste. Scatter olives over plates and place a generous spoonful of herb mayonnaise in center of each plate. Serve salad with remaining mayonnaise on the side, if desired.

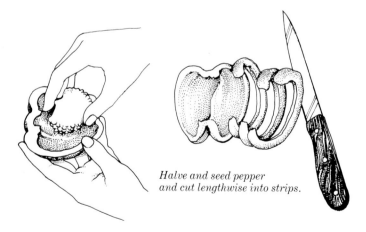

Halve and seed pepper and cut lengthwise into strips.

Herb Mayonnaise

Selection of fresh herbs, such as parsley, chives, chervil, tarragon, or marjoram
Medium-size clove garlic
1 lemon, or 1 tablespoon tarragon vinegar
1 egg, at room temperature
¼ teaspoon salt
⅔ cup olive, peanut, or vegetable oil
Freshly ground pepper

1. Wash herbs and dry with paper towels. Remove stems and discard. Finely chop enough herbs to measure ¼ cup; set aside.

2. Crush garlic under flat blade of chef's knife and remove peel; chop very finely and set aside.

3. Halve lemon crosswise and squeeze enough juice to measure 1 tablespoon.

4. Separate egg, placing yolk in medium-size bowl and reserving white for another use.

5. To keep bowl stationary, set it on folded kitchen towel. Add 1 teaspoon lemon juice or vinegar and salt to yolk, and whisk to combine.

6. Whisking constantly, add oil, drop by drop, until one-third of the oil has been incorporated; continue whisking until mayonnaise is thick and smooth. Thin with a little more lemon juice or vinegar and resume adding oil, 1 spoonful at a time, whisking after each addition until oil is completely incorporated before adding more.

7. When all the oil has been incorporated, thin mayonnaise to desired consistency with hot water, whisking in a drop at a time. Stir in herbs and garlic. Adjust seasoning by adding more lemon juice, vinegar, or salt, if necessary. Thin again, if needed, stir in a few twists of pepper, and set aside until ready to serve.

Goat Cheese with Rosemary, Black Pepper, and Olive Oil

12-ounce log goat cheese, such as Montrachet (without ash), or round chèvre
2 to 3 sprigs fresh rosemary, plus 3 sprigs for garnish (optional), or 1 to 2 teaspoons dried
Freshly ground black pepper
2 tablespoons extra-virgin olive oil

1. Check surface of goat cheese and scrape away any discoloration with back of paring knife.

2. If using fresh rosemary, strip enough leaves from stems to measure about 2 teaspoons; chop finely. Sprinkle cheese with fresh or dried rosemary and pat gently to help herb adhere.

3. Coarsely grind black pepper over cheese and pat gently.

4. Place goat cheese on serving platter and drizzle with 1 tablespoon olive oil; set aside.

5. Just before serving, drizzle goat cheese with remaining olive oil. Garnish platter with sprigs of rosemary, if desired.

Sugar Snap Pea Soup
Tofu and Vegetable Salad with
Mustard-Shallot Mayonnaise

Tofu and vegetable salad looks elegant nestled in radicchio leaves surrounded by vegetables, olives, and cornichons. With the salad, serve sugar snap pea soup and slices of whole-grain bread if desired.

Sugar snap peas, like Chinese snow peas, are crisp and sweet with an edible pod. You can buy them at good greengrocers for a limited time in the spring; at other times, use snow peas. In either case, buy bright unblemished pods with thin green skins. They will keep for a day in a plastic bag in the refrigerator; wash them just before preparing the soup.

When tofu is packed in water, you must squeeze out the liquid before use. The traditional method is to wrap the tofu in a dish towel, placing a weight on top to press out the water, but this can take more than an hour. You can shorten the time, as this cook does, by putting the tofu in a kitchen towel and twisting it to squeeze out excess water.

Cornichons, tiny French pickled gherkins, are a tart garnish for the tofu salad platter. Look for them at specialty food shops. They can be refrigerated in their liquid for up to six months.

WHAT TO DRINK

In keeping with the light character of this meal, the cook suggests serving iced apple juice or white grape juice. A simple fruity white wine, such as Soave or Orvieto, would also be appropriate.

SHOPPING LIST AND STAPLES

1½ blocks firm tofu (about 1½ pounds total weight)
1 pound sugar snap peas or snow peas
1 head red leaf or romaine lettuce
1 head radicchio
1 pint cherry tomatoes
1 large cucumber
Small red or green bell pepper
Small carrot
Small bunch celery
Small red onion
1 bunch scallions
3 to 4 large shallots
Small bunch fresh chives
Selection of fresh herbs, such as parsley, thyme, basil, marjoram, or oregano
1 lemon (optional)
1 egg
2 tablespoons unsalted butter
⅔ cup peanut or olive oil
1 to 2 teaspoons sherry vinegar or other strong vinegar

1 teaspoon white wine vinegar, approximately, plus
   1 tablespoon (if not using lemon)
1 to 2 tablespoons Dijon mustard
11-ounce can black or green olives
7-ounce jar cornichons or sliced vinegar pickles
2-ounce jar capers
¼ teaspoon Cayenne pepper
Salt
Freshly ground pepper

UTENSILS

Blender or food processor
Medium-size heavy-gauge saucepan
Large bowl
2 medium-size bowls
Salad spinner (optional)
Colander
Fine sieve
Small strainer
Measuring cups and spoons
Chef's knife
Paring knife
Wooden spoon
Metal spoon
Rubber spatula
Small whisk
Vegetable peeler

START-TO-FINISH STEPS

Thirty minutes ahead: Set out egg to come to room temperature for mayonnaise recipe.

1. Wash fresh herbs and pat dry with paper towels. Trim stems and discard. Snip enough chives to measure 2 tablespoons for soup recipe; reserve remainder for another use. Finely chop enough mixed herbs to measure 2 to 3 tablespoons for salad recipe; reserve remainder for another use.
2. Follow soup recipe steps 1 through 4.
3. While soup is coming to a boil, follow mayonnaise recipe steps 1 through 3.
4. Follow soup recipe step 5 and mayonnaise recipe steps 4 through 6.
5. Follow soup recipe step 6 and salad recipe steps 1 through 7.
6. Follow soup recipe steps 7 and 8.
7. Follow salad recipe steps 8 through 12.
8. Follow soup recipe steps 9 through 11 and serve as first course.
9. Follow salad recipe step 13 and serve.

RECIPES

Sugar Snap Pea Soup

2 tablespoons unsalted butter
1 bunch scallions

1 pound sugar snap peas or snow peas
Salt
1 teaspoon white wine vinegar, approximately
2 tablespoons snipped fresh chives
Freshly ground pepper

1. Heat butter and ½ cup water in medium-size heavy-gauge saucepan over medium-low heat.
2. While butter is melting, rinse scallions and dry with paper towels. Trim ends and remove any bruised or limp green parts. Cut scallions crosswise into ½-inch-long pieces to measure about 1¼ cups. Add scallions to pan and cook gently, stirring occasionally, 5 minutes.
3. While scallions are cooking, place peas in colander and rinse thoroughly under cold running water. Remove and discard any bad peas. Without removing strings or stems, chop coarsely. Add peas to scallions and cook, turning them to coat with butter, about 2 minutes.
4. Add 4 cups cold water and 1 teaspoon salt to pan, and slowly bring soup to a boil, uncovered, over medium heat.
5. As soon as soup comes to a boil, lower heat and simmer gently 5 minutes.
6. Remove soup from heat and set aside to cool slightly.
7. Transfer soup to blender and purée at least 1 minute on highest speed. Or, in batches, purée in food processor.
8. Pour soup through fine sieve set over medium-size bowl, pressing with back of spoon to force any remaining solid bits through. Return soup to pan; set aside.
9. Place pan over low heat just until soup is heated through; do *not* boil.
10. Taste soup and adjust seasoning by adding a few drops of vinegar or some salt, if desired.
11. Divide soup among 4 bowls and serve garnished with snipped chives and freshly ground pepper.

Tofu and Vegetable Salad with Mustard-Shallot Mayonnaise

1½ blocks firm tofu (about 1½ pounds total weight)
1 stalk celery
Small red or green bell pepper
Small carrot
1 tablespoon capers
2 to 3 tablespoons finely chopped mixed fresh herbs, such as chives, parsley, thyme, basil, marjoram, or oregano
Mustard-Shallot Mayonnaise (see following recipe)
1 to 2 teaspoons sherry vinegar or other strong vinegar
¼ teaspoon Cayenne pepper
Freshly ground pepper
Salt
1 head red leaf or romaine lettuce
1 head radicchio
1 pint cherry tomatoes
1 large cucumber
Small red onion
11-ounce can black or green olives
7-ounce jar cornichons or sliced vinegar pickles

1. Rinse tofu under cold water and break in large pieces.

Place tofu on kitchen towel, gather ends of towel together, and twist, squeezing tofu to remove excess moisture.

2. Turn tofu into large bowl and break into small pieces. It should resemble large-curd cottage cheese.

3. Rinse and dry celery. Slice lengthwise into strips, then dice to measure about ¼ cup. Add celery to tofu.

4. Rinse bell pepper and dry with paper towel. Halve, core, and seed pepper. Cut pepper lengthwise into ¼-inch-wide strips, then cut strips crosswise into small pieces to measure about ¼ cup. Add bell pepper to tofu.

5. Peel and trim carrot. Cut on diagonal into ¼-inch-thick slices; stack slices and cut into matchsticks. Gather matchsticks together and cut them crosswise into fine dice. Add carrot to tofu.

6. Drain and rinse capers. Chop coarsely and add to tofu.

7. Add fresh herbs to tofu and, using rubber spatula, fold chopped ingredients into tofu to combine. Add ¼ cup mustard-shallot mayonnaise, 1 to 2 teaspoons sherry vinegar, Cayenne, and pepper to taste, and fold into salad. Adjust seasoning by adding salt, vinegar, or Cayenne; as the salad rests, its flavors will blend and intensify.

8. Wash and dry lettuce and radicchio. Remove and discard any bruised or discolored outer leaves. Line 4 dinner plates with lettuce. Using 2 leaves of radicchio for each plate, nest end of 1 leaf inside of the other to form a bowl and place bowl in center of each plate. Cover with plastic wrap and refrigerate until ready to serve.

9. Wash tomatoes and dry with paper towels.

10. Wash cucumber and dry with paper towel. Cut crosswise into ⅛-inch-thick slices.

11. Peel onion and cut crosswise into ⅛-inch-thick slices.

12. Drain olives and cornichons, if using.

13. Taste and re-season tofu, if desired. Spoon tofu salad into each radicchio bowl and garnish plate with tomatoes, cucumber, onion, olives, and cornichons. Drizzle remaining mustard-shallot dressing over tofu and serve.

Mustard-Shallot Mayonnaise

3 to 4 large shallots
1 lemon or 1 tablespoon white wine vinegar
1 egg, at room temperature
Salt
⅔ cup peanut or olive oil
1 to 2 tablespoons Dijon mustard
Freshly ground pepper

1. Peel and finely chop enough shallots to measure ¼ cup; set aside.

2. If using lemon, halve and squeeze enough juice to measure ½ tablespoon.

3. Separate egg, placing yolk in medium-size bowl and reserving white for another use.

4. Add ¼ teaspoon salt and 1 teaspoon lemon juice or vinegar to yolk, and whisk until blended.

5. Whisking constantly, add oil, drop by drop, until one-third of the oil has been incorporated and continue whisking until mayonnaise is thick and smooth. Thin with a teaspoon of lemon juice or vinegar and resume adding

oil 1 spoonful at a time, whisking after each addition until completely incorporated before adding more.

6. When all the oil has been incorporated, thin mayonnaise to desired consistency with hot water, whisking in a drop at a time. Then fold in shallots and 1 tablespoon mustard. Adjust seasoning; set aside until ready to use.

ADDED TOUCH

The lemon flavor of these puffy cookies is accented by the sweet lemony glaze. This recipe makes about 20 cookies and enough glaze to just cover each. Double the glaze ingredients if you want more.

Glazed Lemon Cookies

1 lemon
4 tablespoons unsalted butter
¼ cup cream cheese, at room temperature
⅓ cup sugar
1 egg yolk
1 cup all-purpose flour
½ teaspoon baking powder
¼ teaspoon salt
4-ounce can shelled nuts, such as pistachios, walnuts, or almonds
½ cup confectioners' sugar

1. Rinse lemon and dry with paper towel. Using zester or grater, remove rind, avoiding as much white pith as possible. Squeeze enough juice to measure 2½ tablespoons; set aside.

2. In large bowl, combine butter, cream cheese, and sugar, and cream together with wooden spoon until well blended and fluffy.

3. Add egg yolk, lemon zest, and 1 tablespoon lemon juice, and stir until well blended.

4. Combine flour, baking powder, and salt in medium-size bowl. Sift dry ingredients into butter mixture and combine, using wooden spoon.

5. Gather dough into a ball, wrap in plastic, and refrigerate at least 1 hour, or until dough is firm and easy to handle.

6. Preheat oven to 375 degrees.

7. When ready to bake, break off pieces of dough about the size of a small walnut and roll between palms into balls. Place balls a few inches apart on ungreased cookie sheet and flatten each ball with the bottom of a glass. If the dough becomes warm and the glass sticks, dip bottom of glass in some flour and then press cookies flat.

8. Bake cookies in middle of oven 10 to 12 minutes, or until nicely browned on bottom but light on top.

9. While cookies are baking, finely chop nuts; set aside.

10. For glaze, place remaining lemon juice in wide shallow bowl. Sift confectioners' sugar over lemon juice, then stir until smooth and creamy.

11. Remove cookies from oven and spread glaze over each warm cookie with flat metal pastry spatula.

12. While glaze is still wet, sprinkle nuts over cookies and place on metal racks to cool.

Anne Lindsay Greer

S outhwestern cooking, with its Mexican and Spanish roots, is piquant, earthy fare characterized by the use of chilies, corn, rice, beans, and avocados. Anne Lindsay Greer, who has lived in the Southwest for many years, has a deep respect for the region's traditional cuisine, but she also likes to create variations on those dishes. For her, salad making is an ideal way to lighten heavy recipes and to combine ingredients that might seem to be at odds with one another.

In Menu 1, for example, she mixes corn, rice, and pistachio nuts with a white wine vinaigrette to make a flavorful base for smoked turkey, sausage, and slices of cantaloupe. As a follow-up to this colorful combination, she serves a delicious dessert of baked goat cheese with raspberry sauce.

Menus 2 and 3 are more typical south-of-the-border meals. Menu 2 features *sangrita*, a spicy drink that the cook calls a cross between gazpacho and a Bloody Mary without the liquor. *Serrano* chilies give it a fiery punch. The warm chicken salad entrée is also flavored with chilies—the milder Anaheim variety—and is garnished with crisp tortilla strips and avocado balls.

Menu 3 proves that not all Mexican food need be spicy. In Anne Lindsay Greer's light *seviche*, a dish that traditionally consists of marinated raw fish, the scallops are simply tossed with red, green, and yellow bell peppers. With the *seviche*, the cook offers *quesadillas*, or fried tortilla turnovers, filled with spinach and two kinds of cheese. A dessert of pineapple and orange slices is the finale.

For a festive Tex-Mex meal, serve portions of this flavorful salad on unusual platters. Baked goat cheese with raspberry sauce is the refreshing dessert.

Smoked Meat and Pistachio Rice Salad
Baked Goat Cheese with Raspberry Sauce

For the dessert, scoops of goat cheese are dipped into beaten egg, then covered with a sweet nut and bread crumb mixture prior to baking. This protective coating seals the cheese and prevents it from melting too much at the high baking temperature. Some imported goat cheeses are too strong and dense for this recipe, so select a mild, creamy domestic variety or a mild imported type such as French Capricette.

WHAT TO DRINK

The variety of flavors in this meal demands a crisp white wine. A light, fruity California Chenin Blanc is the cook's suggestion. Look for one that is fully dry.

SHOPPING LIST AND STAPLES

¾ pound smoked turkey breast
½ pound fully cooked smoked sausage
2 ears fresh corn, or 10-ounce package frozen kernels
1 bunch watercress
1 bunch scallions
Small ripe cantaloupe or papaya
½ pint fresh raspberries, or 10-ounce package frozen
    unsweetened raspberries, or 1 ripe mango
Large egg
2 tablespoons unsalted butter
¾ pound mild domestic or imported goat cheese
3 tablespoons safflower oil
2 tablespoons vegetable oil
2 tablespoons white wine vinegar
2 tablespoons maple syrup, approximately
¼ cup all-purpose flour
½ cup long-grain rice
2 slices home-style white bread
6 tablespoons sugar
2-ounce jar pine nuts
2-ounce package raw shelled pistachio nuts
½ teaspoon dry mustard
Salt and freshly ground black pepper

UTENSILS

Blender
Medium-size heavy-gauge skillet
Medium-size heavy-gauge saucepan with cover
Small heavy-gauge saucepan
Baking sheet
9-inch pie pan or shallow plate
Large bowl
3 small bowls
Salad spinner (optional)
Measuring cups and spoons
Chef's knife
Paring knife
Strainer
2 wooden spoons
Metal spatula
Whisk
Ice cream scoop (optional)

START-TO-FINISH STEPS

One hour ahead: If using frozen corn for salad recipe or frozen raspberries for baked goat cheese recipe, set out to thaw.

1. Follow salad recipe steps 1 through 14.
2. Follow goat cheese recipe steps 1 through 3.
3. Follow salad recipe step 15.
4. Follow goat cheese recipe steps 4 and 5.
5. Follow salad recipe steps 16 and 17, and serve.
6. Follow goat cheese recipe steps 6 through 9 and serve as dessert.

RECIPES

Smoked Meat and Pistachio Rice Salad

Salt
½ pound fully cooked smoked sausage
½ cup long-grain rice
⅓ cup raw shelled pistachio nuts
3 tablespoons safflower oil
2 tablespoons white wine vinegar
½ teaspoon dry mustard
Freshly ground black pepper
1 bunch watercress
6 scallions
2 ears fresh corn, or 10-ounce package frozen
    kernels, thawed
2 tablespoons vegetable oil
¾ pound smoked turkey breast
Small ripe cantaloupe or papaya

1. Preheat oven to 350 degrees.

2. In medium-size heavy-gauge saucepan, combine 1 cup water and ½ teaspoon salt, and bring to a boil over medium-high heat.

3. While water is heating, cut sausage crosswise into ¼-inch-thick slices. Place sausage on large rectangular sheet of foil, gather long edges together, and fold twice to seal. Repeat with short ends to form envelope and place on baking sheet.

4. Add rice to boiling water. When water returns to a boil, stir rice. Reduce heat, cover pan, and simmer gently 15 minutes, or until water is absorbed and rice is tender.

5. While rice is cooking, arrange nuts in single layer on baking sheet with foil-wrapped sausage and bake 10 minutes.

6. Meanwhile, combine safflower oil, vinegar, dry mustard, and salt and pepper to taste in small bowl, and whisk until blended; set aside.

7. Wash watercress and dry in salad spinner or with paper towels. Remove and discard stems. Wrap in paper towels and refrigerate.

8. Wash scallions and dry with paper towels. Trim off ends and discard. Thinly slice scallions; set aside.

9. If using fresh corn, remove husks and silk. With chef's knife, trim off stem so that upended ear will stand flat on work surface. Holding ear of corn upright, press base against surface and, with chef's knife, cut off kernels by pressing blade against cob and slicing downward. Turn ear and repeat process until all kernels are removed. Repeat for remaining ear. Set aside.

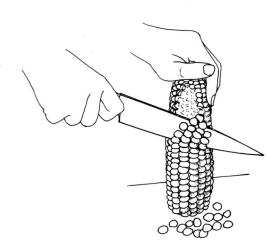

10. Remove sausage and nuts from oven, open foil envelope, and set aside sausage and nuts to cool. Raise oven temperature to 400 degrees. Rinse and dry baking sheet.

11. Remove rice from heat and fluff with fork. Spread rice out on platter, cover with plastic wrap, and place in freezer to chill.

12. Heat vegetable oil in medium-size heavy-gauge skillet over medium-high heat. Add corn and scallions, and sauté, stirring occasionally, 2 to 3 minutes, or until corn is tender.

13. While corn and scallions are cooking, cut turkey breast into ½-inch-wide strips; set aside.

14. Remove corn and scallions from heat and set aside to cool.

15. Combine chilled rice, corn and scallion mixture, roasted nuts, vinaigrette, and salt and pepper to taste in large bowl, and toss with 2 wooden spoons to combine. Cover with plastic wrap and refrigerate until ready to serve.

16. If using cantaloupe, halve, scoop out seeds and discard. Cut one half lengthwise into 8 crescents; reserve remaining half for another use. If using papaya, halve lengthwise; scoop out seeds and discard. Cut one half lengthwise into 8 slices; peel each slice. Reserve remaining half for another use.

17. Divide rice mixture among 4 dinner plates. Top each serving with equal portions of baked sausage and turkey strips. Arrange watercress around sausage. Place 2 slices of cantaloupe or papaya on each plate and serve.

Baked Goat Cheese with Raspberry Sauce

2 slices home-style white bread
6 tablespoons sugar
½ cup pine nuts
½ pint fresh raspberries, or 10-ounce package
    frozen unsweetened raspberries, thawed, or 1 ripe
    mango
1 to 2 tablespoons maple syrup
Large egg
¼ cup all-purpose flour
¾ pound mild domestic or imported goat cheese
2 tablespoons unsalted butter

1. Trim crusts from bread; tear bread into pieces. Combine bread, sugar, and pine nuts in blender and grind coarsely. Transfer mixture to pie pan or shallow plate; set aside.

2. If using fresh raspberries, gently rinse under cold running water. Transfer to double thickness of paper towels and pat dry. If using mango, halve lengthwise. Using knife, loosen pit from one half, then gently pull mango apart. Cut around and under pit; remove and discard. Cut each half lengthwise into quarters; peel each slice by running knife between rind and flesh.

3. Combine fruit and maple syrup to taste in blender and purée. If using raspberries, force purée through strainer set over small bowl to remove seeds; set aside.

4. Break egg into small bowl and beat lightly. Place flour on sheet of waxed paper.

5. Using ice cream scoop or deep spoon, shape goat cheese into rounds. Dust rounds lightly with flour, dip in egg, and then roll in crumb mixture until thoroughly coated. Transfer to baking sheet. Repeat with remaining rounds. Set aside.

6. When ready to serve dessert, melt butter in small heavy-gauge saucepan over low heat.

7. Drizzle cheese rounds with melted butter and bake in 400-degree oven 8 to 10 minutes, or until golden.

8. Meanwhile, divide fruit purée among 4 small dessert bowls.

9. Using metal spatula, transfer baked cheese rounds to bowls with fruit purée and serve.

Sangrita
Mexican Chicken Salad

Warm chicken salad with tortilla strips and avocado balls goes well with a spicy mug of well-chilled sangrita.

Corn tortillas, the flat bread of Mexico, are made of *masa harina*, a flour made from dried corn kernels treated with lime. Available fresh in the dairy department of most supermarkets, corn tortillas should be stored in plastic wrap in the refrigerator or freezer.

Avocado balls garnish the main-course chicken salad. A perfectly ripe avocado is slightly soft to the touch with no bruises or dark spots on the skin. To test for ripeness, stick a toothpick into the stem end; if it goes in and out easily, the avocado is ready to eat. An immature avocado will ripen within a day or two if placed in a brown paper bag and left at room temperature. A ripe avocado keeps for three to five days in the refrigerator.

WHAT TO DRINK

Ice-cold beer, especially a dark, full-flavored brand from Mexico, would be good with this menu, if you want to serve another beverage besides the *sangrita*.

SHOPPING LIST AND STAPLES

2 boneless, skinless chicken breasts, halved (about 1¼ pounds total weight)
1 head iceberg lettuce
¼ pound spinach
2 large avocados
2 fresh Anaheim chilies, or 4-ounce can whole mild green chilies
1 or 2 fresh serrano chilies, or 4-ounce can
Small yellow onion
1 clove garlic
2 medium-size lemons
2 limes, plus 1 additional for garnish (optional)
2 oranges, plus 1 additional for garnish (optional)
28-ounce can Italian plum tomatoes
8-ounce can tomato juice
¼ pound Monterey Jack cheese
3 fresh corn tortillas, or 1 package frozen
1 cup peanut oil
3 tablespoons vegetable oil, approximately
3 tablespoons white wine vinegar
1 tablespoon sugar
1 teaspoon dry mustard
Salt and freshly ground black and white pepper

UTENSILS

Food processor (optional)
Blender
Medium-size skillet
Small heavy-gauge saucepan
1 baking sheet, plus 1 additional (optional)
2 medium-size bowls
1 small bowl
Measuring cups and spoons
Chef's knife
Paring knife
2 wooden spoons
Slotted spatula or mesh strainer
Metal tongs
Long-handled double-pronged fork
Melon baller
Deep-fat thermometer
Juicer
Grater (if not using processor)
Brown paper bag

START-TO-FINISH STEPS

Thirty minutes ahead: If using frozen tortillas for salad recipe, set out to thaw.

1. Follow sangrita recipe steps 1 through 8.
2. Follow salad recipe steps 1 through 18.
3. Follow sangrita recipe step 9 and serve with salad.

RECIPES

Sangrita

28-ounce can Italian plum tomatoes
Small yellow onion
1 or 2 fresh or canned serrano chilies
2 oranges, plus 1 additional for garnish (optional)
2 limes, plus 1 additional for garnish (optional)
Medium-size lemon
1 tablespoon sugar
8-ounce can tomato juice
Salt and freshly ground black pepper

1. Seed tomatoes, reserving liquid; set aside.
2. Peel and halve onion. Coarsely chop one half; reserve remaining half for another use.
3. Wearing rubber gloves, trim stems from fresh chilies, if using. Split chilies lengthwise; with tip of knife, remove seeds and discard. Chop coarsely. If using canned chilies, rinse under cold water and dry; proceed as for fresh.
4. Squeeze enough fruits to measure about 1 cup orange juice, about ¼ cup lime juice, and ¼ cup lemon juice.
5. Combine tomatoes, their reserved liquid, onion, chilies to taste, sugar, and tomato juice in blender and purée.
6. Add fruit juices to purée and blend.
7. Season sangrita with salt and pepper to taste, cover container, and refrigerate until ready to serve.
8. Wash and dry additional orange and lime, if using for garnish. Cut four thin slices from each, wrap in plastic, and refrigerate until ready to serve.
9. Divide sangrita among 4 mugs and garnish each mug with an orange and a lime slice, if desired.

Mexican Chicken Salad

3 fresh corn tortillas, or 3 frozen, thawed
2 fresh Anaheim chilies, or 4-ounce can whole mild green chilies
1 cup peanut oil

1 head iceberg lettuce
¼ pound spinach
1 clove garlic
1 teaspoon dry mustard
3 tablespoons white wine vinegar
Salt and freshly ground white pepper
Medium-size lemon
2 large avocados
¼ pound Monterey Jack cheese
2 boneless, skinless chicken breasts, halved
   (about 1¼ pounds total weight)
3 tablespoons vegetable oil, approximately

1. Stack tortillas and cut into ½-inch-wide by 2-inch-long strips. Spread out strips in single layer on cookie sheet to dry.
2. Meanwhile, if using fresh chilies, spear through top with long-handled double-pronged fork and hold directly over flame of gas burner, or place on foil-lined baking sheet about 4 inches from heating element in broiler and turn to char skins evenly. Place chilies in paper bag, close, and set aside to steam 10 to 20 minutes.
3. Heat peanut oil in small heavy-gauge saucepan over medium-high heat until deep-fat thermometer registers 375 degrees.
4. While oil is heating, line platter with double thickness of paper towels.
5. Add one third of tortilla strips to hot oil and fry 20 to 30 seconds, or until crisp, being careful not to burn them. With slotted spatula, transfer strips to paper-towel-lined platter to drain. Repeat with remaining strips.
6. Halve and core lettuce, reserving one half for another use. Rinse remaining half under cold running water and dry with paper towels. Cut crosswise into ½-inch-wide strips and place in medium-size bowl.
7. Wash spinach thoroughly in several changes of cold water and dry with paper towels. Remove and discard tough stems and any bruised or discolored leaves. Stack leaves and cut crosswise into ½-inch-wide strips to make 3 cups. Add to bowl with lettuce, cover with plastic wrap, and refrigerate until ready to serve.
8. Wearing rubber gloves, remove chilies from bag and, holding each chili under cold running water, gently rub to remove charred skin; pat dry with paper towels. Halve, core, and seed chilies. If using canned chilies, turn into strainer and rinse under cold running water; drain. Cut chilies lengthwise into ¼-inch-wide strips; set aside.
9. Peel and mince garlic.
10. For vinaigrette, combine garlic, dry mustard, vinegar, ¼ teaspoon salt, and pepper to taste in small bowl and stir with fork to combine; set aside.
11. Squeeze lemon and pour juice into medium-size bowl.
12. Halve avocados lengthwise; separate by twisting halves in opposite directions. Remove and discard pits. Using small end of melon baller, scoop out flesh. Add avocado balls to lemon juice and toss until evenly coated; set aside.
13. Using food processor fitted with shredding disk or

grater, shred enough cheese to measure ¾ cup; set aside.
14. Divide greens among 4 dinner plates; set aside.
15. Rinse chicken pieces under cold running water and dry with paper towels. Cut chicken into ½-inch-wide by 2-inch-long strips and season with salt and pepper to taste.
16. In medium-size skillet, heat 2 tablespoons vegetable oil over medium-high heat. Add chicken strips and stir fry, drizzling in additional oil to prevent sticking if necessary, 2 to 3 minutes, or until chicken is opaque.
17. Add chilies and vinaigrette, and stir fry another 2 minutes.
18. Divide chicken mixture among plates with lettuce and spinach. Top with grated cheese and garnish each serving with avocado balls and tortilla strips.

ADDED TOUCH

Scalloping the edges of the tortillas with scissors before frying makes the cups more decorative.

Cinnamon Tortilla Cups with Whipped Cream and Berries

1 pint fresh berries, such as blackberries, strawberries,
   blueberries, or raspberries
4 flour tortillas
2 to 3 cups peanut oil
1½ teaspoons cinnamon
1½ cups plus 3 tablespoons sugar
1 cup heavy cream
1 teaspoon vanilla extract

1. Place medium-size bowl and beaters for whipping cream in freezer to chill.
2. Place berries in colander and rinse under cold running water; pat dry with paper towels. Remove and discard any bruised or discolored berries. Reserve 8 to 12 whole berries for garnish. If using strawberries, hull and halve. If using other berries, leave whole.
3. Using kitchen scissors, cut edges of each tortilla into scallop pattern; set aside.
4. In small heavy-gauge saucepan, heat 2 cups oil over medium-high heat until deep-fat thermometer registers 375 degrees.
5. While oil is heating, combine cinnamon and 1½ cups sugar on shallow plate and stir with fork to blend.
6. Line another plate with paper towels.
7. Using metal tongs, press 1 tortilla into hot oil, holding center down to form cup shape, and fry 30 to 45 seconds; transfer to paper-towel-lined plate to drain. Repeat with remaining tortillas, adding more oil if necessary.
8. Carefully coat tortilla cups with cinnamon-sugar mixture and divide among 4 dessert plates; set aside.
9. In chilled bowl, beat heavy cream with electric mixer until soft peaks form. Gently fold in 3 tablespoons sugar and 1 teaspoon vanilla.
10. Fold berries into whipped cream and divide mixture among tortilla cups. Garnish each serving with reserved whole berries and serve.

Seviche with Bell Pepper Strips
Spinach and Cheese Quesadillas
Oranges and Pineapples Mexicano

The tangy scallop salad, spinach and cheese quesadillas, *and marinated fruit dessert will tempt anyone's palate.*

Bay scallops are about half an inch in diameter with pinkish-ivory flesh. When very fresh, scallops have a clean sea-air aroma and appear translucent; avoid any that smell sour or are opaque. If you are not sure that the scallops you have purchased are very fresh, you should blanch them first before marinating them.

WHAT TO DRINK

The cook suggests iced tea, but a white wine sangria would also complement this Mexican menu.

SHOPPING LIST AND STAPLES

1½ pounds bay scallops
1 head Boston lettuce
1 bunch watercress
¼ pound spinach
1 green, 1 red, and 1 yellow bell pepper
Small yellow onion
Small bunch coriander
5 limes
2 seedless oranges
1 juice orange
1 ripe pineapple (about 3 pounds)
4 tablespoons unsalted butter, approximately
½ pound mild domestic or imported goat cheese
¼ pound Monterey Jack cheese
3 tablespoons safflower oil
2 tablespoons vegetable oil
2 tablespoons white wine vinegar
4 fresh flour tortillas, or 1 package frozen
2-ounce jar pine nuts
Salt and freshly ground white pepper
3 tablespoons Triple Sec or other orange-flavored liqueur
1 tablespoon tequila

UTENSILS

Medium-size skillet
Small heavy-gauge skillet
Ovenproof platter
Large nonaluminum bowl
2 medium-size bowls, 1 nonaluminum
Small nonaluminum bowl
Colander

101

Measuring cups and spoons
Chef's knife
Paring knife
2 wooden spoons
Slotted spoon
Metal spatula
Juicer
Grater

START-TO-FINISH STEPS

Thirty minutes ahead: If using frozen tortillas for quesadillas, set out at room temperature to thaw.

1. Follow seviche recipe steps 1 through 6.
2. Follow dessert recipe steps 1 through 3.
3. Follow quesadillas recipe steps 1 through 11.
4. Follow seviche recipe steps 7 through 9.
5. Follow quesadillas recipe steps 12 and 13, and serve with seviche.
6. Follow dessert recipe step 4 and serve.

RECIPES

Seviche with Bell Pepper Strips

5 limes
1 juice orange
1½ pounds bay scallops
1 tablespoon unsalted butter
¼ cup pine nuts
1 green, 1 red, and 1 yellow bell pepper
1 head Boston lettuce
1 bunch watercress
3 tablespoons safflower oil
2 tablespoons white wine vinegar
Salt and freshly ground white pepper

1. Squeeze limes to measure about 1 cup juice and orange to measure ½ cup juice; combine juices in small non-aluminum bowl.
2. Rinse scallops in colander; dry with paper towels.
3. Add scallops to citrus juices, cover with plastic wrap, and refrigerate, turning scallops occasionally, about 30 minutes, or until ready to serve.
4. Melt butter in small heavy-gauge skillet over medium heat. Add pine nuts and sauté, stirring occasionally, 2 to 3 minutes, or until light golden. Set aside.
5. Wash and dry peppers; core, halve, and seed. Cut into ¼-inch-wide by 1½-inch-long strips; set aside.
6. Wash and dry greens. Cut lettuce crosswise into ¼-inch-wide strips. Place greens in medium-size bowl, cover, and refrigerate until ready to serve.
7. For vinaigrette, combine oil, vinegar, and salt and pepper to taste in medium-size nonaluminum bowl and beat with fork until blended.
8. Drain scallops and add to vinaigrette; toss gently to combine. Add pepper strips and toss to combine.
9. Divide greens among 4 dinner plates, top with seviche and peppers, and garnish each serving with pine nuts.

Spinach and Cheese Quesadillas

4 fresh flour tortillas, or 4 frozen, thawed
¼ pound spinach
Small bunch coriander
Small yellow onion
¼ pound Monterey Jack cheese
½ pound mild domestic or imported goat cheese
3 tablespoons unsalted butter, approximately
Salt and freshly ground white pepper
2 tablespoons vegetable oil

1. Preheat oven to 200 degrees.
2. Stack tortillas, wrap in foil, and keep warm in oven.
3. Wash spinach thoroughly and dry. Remove tough stems. Finely chop enough spinach to measure 2 cups.
4. Wash and dry coriander. Trim stems and discard. Finely chop enough coriander to measure 1 tablespoon.
5. Halve, peel, and finely chop enough onion to measure ¼ cup.
6. Using grater, shred enough Monterey Jack to measure ½ cup; reserve remainder for another use. Crumble enough goat cheese to measure 1½ cups; set aside.
7. In medium-size skillet, melt 2 tablespoons butter over medium heat. Add onion and sauté, stirring occasionally, 3 to 4 minutes, or until soft and translucent.
8. Add spinach and cook, stirring, another minute. Remove pan from heat.
9. Add coriander, Monterey Jack, goat cheese, and salt and pepper to taste to spinach, and stir to combine.
10. Remove tortillas from oven. Spread one half of each tortilla with spinach-cheese mixture; fold over free half. Rinse and dry skillet.
11. Line ovenproof platter with paper towels.
12. Heat 1 teaspoon butter and 1 teaspoon oil in medium-size skillet over medium-high heat. One at a time, fry quesadillas 1 minute per side, or until golden brown, adding more butter and oil as necessary to prevent sticking. Transfer quesadillas to paper-towel-lined platter and keep warm in oven until ready to serve.
13. Just before serving, cut quesadillas in half.

Oranges and Pineapples Mexicano

1 ripe pineapple (about 3 pounds)
2 seedless oranges
3 tablespoons Triple Sec or other orange-flavored liqueur
1 tablespoon tequila

1. With chef's knife, cut ¾-inch slice from top and bottom of pineapple, and discard. Cut pineapple lengthwise into quarters. Remove woody core from quarters and discard. Slide a thin-bladed knife between flesh and rind, and lift out flesh. Cut crosswise into ½-inch-thick slices and place in large nonaluminum bowl.
2. Peel oranges, removing as much white pith as possible, over bowl with pineapple; cut to separate sections.
3. Add liqueur and tequila to fruit and toss to combine; cover and set aside to marinate at least 30 minutes.
4. Divide fruit among 4 dessert bowls and serve.

Acknowledgments

The Editors would like to thank the following for their courtesy in lending items for photography: *Cover:* flatware—Gorham; plate—Oleksa Collection; wicker tray—Pan American Phoenix. *Frontispiece:* baskets—Be Seated. *Pages 16–17:* tablecloth—Conran's; napkin—Leacock & Co. *Pages 20–21:* chopsticks—Five Eggs; platters, plates—Pottery designer Claire Des Becker; countertop—Formica® Brand Laminate by Formica Corp. *Page 23:* tablecloth—Conran's; platters—Pan American Phoenix; bowl—Be Seated. *Pages 26–27:* countertop—Formica® Brand Laminate by Formica Corp.; mugs, platter, vase—Pottery Barn; flatware—The Lauffer Co. *Pages 30–31:* dishes—Conran's. *Page 33:* plate—Conran's; flatware—Gorham. *Pages 36–37:* chopsticks—Five Eggs; dishes—Japan Interiors Gallery; glasses—Gorham. *Page 40:* plates—Fitz & Floyd; glass, napkin—Conran's. *Page 43:* bowl—Conran's; rug, basket—Be Seated. *Pages 46–47:* platters—Terrafirma. *Page 50:* tray—Eigen Arts. *Page 52:* tablecloth—Conran's; fork—The Lauffer Co.; tray, napkin, trivet, bowl—Pottery Barn. *Pages 54–55:* paper surface—Four Hands Bindery; bowl, spoon, chopsticks—Five Eggs; plates—The Museum Store of the Museum of Modern Art. *Page 58:* flatware—Gorham; plate—Dan Levy. *Page 61:* dishes, napkin, tablecloth—Pierre Deux. *Pages 64–65:* plate, platters, tablecloth, napkin—Conran's. *Page 71:* tiles—Terra Design, Inc., Morristown, NJ; flatware—Gorham. *Pages 74–75:* flatware—L.L. Bean; bowl—Oleksa Collection; mat, napkin—Susskind Collection. *Pages 78–79:* teak bowl—Bowl & Board; marble, ladle, bowl—Pottery Barn; mugs—Conran's. *Page 81:* tablecloth, bowls, plates—Conran's; napkins—Fabindia; board—Fran Shinagel; flatware—Gorham. *Pages 84–85:* platter, tureen—Wolfman-Gold & Good Co.; basket—Pottery Barn. *Page 88:* plates, tablecloth—Conran's; checked napkin—St. Remy; tins, cheese board—Slotnick Collection. *Page 91:* soup bowl, salad plate—Ad Hoc Housewares; napkin—Leacock & Co. *Pages 94–95:* plate—Eigen Arts; fork—Wallace Silversmiths. *Page 98:* plate, mug, cloth—Pan American Phoenix; napkin—Susskind Collection. *Page 101:* plate, bowl, rug—Bowl & Board. *Kitchen equipment courtesy of:* White-Westinghouse, Commercial Aluminum Cookware Co., Robot-Coupe, Caloric, Kitchen-Aid, J.A. Henckels Zwillingswerk, Inc., and Schwabel Corp. Microwave oven compliments of Litton Microwave Cooking Products.

Illustrations by Ray Skibinski
Production by Giga Communications

Index